FRAGMENTS OF LIGHT

INSIGHTS, BREAKTHROUGHS & EPIPHANIES

Richard Rudd

GENE KEYS

First edition published in Great Britain and USA 2023
by Gene Keys Publishing Ltd
13 Freeland Park, Wareham Road, Poole BH16 6FA

Richard Rudd

Fragments of Light
Insights, Breakthroughs & Epiphanies

Hardback Print Edition ISBN 978-1-913820-11-4
Kindle Edition ISBN 978-1-913820-13-8

Edited by Juliet Savage

genekeys.com

About The Author

An international teacher, mystic and poet, Richard Rudd attended Edinburgh University where he gained a Master's degree in literature and metaphysics. A born explorer, he has studied with great teachers in the East, traveled through the Himalayas, the Pacific, the Americas and the Arctic. He worked in the film industry in Australia, trained as a teacher of Chi Kung and meditation in Thailand and sailed across the Atlantic Ocean on a small yacht.

Richard's mystical journey began early in life as he experienced strange energies rushing throughout his body. This catalysed his spiritual search. All his studies became synthesised in 2002 when he began to write and receive *The Gene Keys* – a vast synthesis exploring the miraculous possibilities inherent in human DNA.

Today Richard continues to extend and embody the wisdom he receives, sharing it with an ever-growing audience around the world. His work has been translated into many languages, and in 2019, Richard was named on the Watkins list of *The 100 Most Spiritually Influential Living People.*

Table of Fragments

Chapter 1 – The Path of Awakening

Chapter 2 – Alchemy

CHAPTER 3 – THE ART OF CONTEMPLATION

CHAPTER 4 – A NEW FUTURE

CHAPTER 5 – A RELAXING TRUTH

CHAPTER 6 – RIPPLES OF CONSCIOUSNESS

CHAPTER 7 – FINDING THE RADIANCE

CHAPTER 8 – THE GOOD PRAYER

The text of this book has been transcribed from the author's original video series. Although slight changes have been made to the text, we have endeavoured to retain the informal flow, style and cadence of the original oral transmission.

FOREWORD

One of the most effective ways of sharing spiritual wisdom is and has always been, through the art of storytelling. Stories, anecdotes, parables, even jokes, all engage our right brain, and that suits the field of wisdom more than the quest of knowledge. The tales in this book are drawn from everyday life – from authors or teachers who have inspired me, from my family, my friends and the rich experience of simply living life. Many of them come from my own pain, which is one of the greatest of teachers. Anyone can unlock wisdom through their life. The secret I have found is the Art of Contemplation. Contemplation is a lens that allows us to continuously digest life experiences and extract the essence from them.

It is out of my own Contemplation that these Fragments have emerged – as Insights, Breakthroughs and Epiphanies. If you read or have already read my little book 'The Art of Contemplation', you will already understand the nature of these three words. Insights detonate through the mind suddenly opening, Breakthroughs appear when the heart shines onto our pain and an emotional transformation occurs, and Epiphanies (the rarest) occur when our entire being and body shudders in an orgasmic state of pure knowing.

The Fragments collected in this book have been beautifully transcribed and edited from their original oral transmissions. My particular thanks go to Juliet Savage for editing and arranging these transcendent tales in such a creative and exquisite form. They cover a wide range of subjects from the mystical to the mundane, forming a kind of fluid autobiography of my inner life over a period of around ten years. In this, they track my personal spiritual evolution as I was laying out the spiritual teachings of the Gene Keys.

If you are a student of the Gene Keys teachings, you may thus find them of interest, for they run parallel to the teachings. You may also read these Fragments and find them helpful without knowing anything about the Gene Keys. They seem to work quite well when used as a kind of Oracle, when one opens the book at a random page. So I hope they offer you some comfort and food for thought.

It has been a very odd experience for me revisiting these stories, as at times I have the distinct feeling that they do not seem to have come from me at all. In many cases I don't even recall saying these things. That in itself is worthy of deeper contemplation.

Whoever you are, and however you came here, I wish you a warm welcome and I hope you find these Fragments insightful and inspiring on your journey into the wisdom within.

Richard Rudd

For Marian, my wife, who has stood beside me during all my best and my worst moments. Thank you beyond words...

THE PATH OF AWAKENING

*The path of awakening is a journey that everyone will
eventually take at some point, even if not within
this lifetime. Just one insight can trigger a moment
of awakening, and with each step another layer
falls away as we open and remember a little more.
The path is made up of many small steps, but
occasionally we will take a giant leap and experience
the transcendence and elation of an epiphany.*

*The world needs fully awakened beings, because only
they can catalyse more and more people to awaken.
I believe that there is no greater service
to humanity than this.*

NO MAN IS AN ISLAND

When John Donne, the English poet, wrote, 'No man is an island,' he was saying that we are all interconnected and that we depend on one another. His words have been used and quoted ever since, although some people nowadays prefer to say, 'No hu-man is an island,' to be politically correct. Donne's point is that we are all connected as we follow life's journey together, even though we are all at different stages on the path of awakening. When you are walking that path, you begin to see at a higher level, and you remember and hear things in a completely different way. You can still relate to people on an everyday level, but when you look at the universe, your worldview opens up and starts to look different. You start seeing things through your heart, and thus you come in time to remember your greater being.

For many of us this can occur while the people around us remain fixed in their worldview, even as ours is changing. This can be very challenging, because it can make you feel very alone. You may even be tempted to think '*I need to move away from all these other people who are still asleep and find people who are on my wavelength*,' which would be absolutely understandable. But this can be a mistake because when you are an instrument of awakening, you are needed most where there are people who aren't necessarily awakening yet, even though this can be a great challenge, and a common one.

For your awakening to become consistently powerful, it needs not to depend on your environment but to be strengthened from within. There is nothing like being surrounded by those who do not share your worldview to help you refine and polish the lens of your awareness. I say this to encourage people whose families perhaps do not awaken, or do not understand them, or perhaps even whose friends are very different and hold very different world views. That is perfectly normal and it can even be rather wonderful.

I spend a lot of my time surrounded by people who do not share my world view, and who do not really know anything about the Gene Keys. Many of them do not know about these spiritual things and are not inspired to know more yet. This doesn't stop you loving them. That is the thing: you can love someone without having to impose your worldview on them. You can just be the field so that you are always ready to have that conversation with them if they want to. If they don't, then you just love them where they are at. You let them learn through their own experiences and suffering, in their own way. In time they will come to their own spiritual views, maybe not in this life, but they will eventually.

You can take comfort from the fact that you are not alone. No man is an island. No woman is an island. You may be placed on an island, and if you are, then you probably have a job to do on that island.

Obviously when we look around, we see that for the most part the world does not share a more spiritual worldview yet – an expansive, open-hearted, truly optimistic worldview. When you look at the world headlines and the world stage for example, you are not seeing the whole picture. You are seeing a tiny fragment that is being endlessly repeated in a negative light.

If you were to see the big picture, if you were to go into the cells of your being, you would see the true memory that everything is woven of light, and that everything is moving from light towards light, through love. If everyone could see that, then the world would be different. One day the world *will* be different.

Yet, for the moment, many people do not see that. They vehemently defend their worldview and they often feel deeply threatened by those who, as they see it, have an idealistic, dreamy or naive New Age worldview. So it's important to relax and realise that this is all quite normal when someone is defending their own worldview.

In summary, I would say to be careful about defending your worldview. Allow it to just permeate the worldviews of others. The moment that someone gets uncomfortable, just be empathic towards them. You do not have to hide what you feel or who you are, but start to listen to others and let their worldview just be what it is. Be the example of the good listener, the one who has eternal patience. It has taken you many lifetimes to be able to start to awaken. Allow others that same grace. In their own time they will come to it. In the meantime, just love them. That in itself will create the field that makes anything possible for them, and for you.

You are not alone. There are many of us, and we are catching fire all across the globe. Soon, in a few hundred years or a few thousand years, the world is going to look very different through the worldview of awakening.

THE UPTIGHT BUDDHA

'The Uptight Buddha' is a mischievous title, and it is inspired partly by a friend of mine, a very awakened being, who happens to have Parkinson's disease. As he observed himself and his Parkinson's, he noticed that it does not affect his journey of awakening in any way, but it makes his body uptight. He has a tightness and a quivering, an energy field that he has inherited in some way. He refers to it as the Uptight Buddha, which I think contains a very deep piece of wisdom. We often think that we have to be perfect, and we think that the field of awakening, or the Buddha principle, is a very blissed-out person sitting in perfect awareness of all that is, and that everything is idyllic. But it is not always that way.

We have to deal with whatever comes along in life, yet, like my friend, it does not have to affect the awakened clarity of our inner nature. This is an important teaching for all of us, for the new aeon, if you like, because we have these expectations of ourselves and therefore of others. Sometimes we expect everyone to be more awake, and super-clear or super-aware or super-moral, but actually we are what we are, and we are just humans.

So it is a really powerful thing to allow yourself permission to be awake in whatever state you are in. You can bring your full attention to the moment, even now while you are reading this. Take some deep breaths and just bring yourself into the present. Right now, in this moment, you are as awake as the most exalted being, as Buddha, as Christ, because you are in perfect presence, with whatever stuff is going through you. This is the Uptight Buddha because, sometimes, we are a rolling passage of consciousness that is unfinished, incomplete, moving and striving towards perfection, and yet we may never get there. If we did get there, what then?

One day, of course, all consciousness will attain that perfection, but then it will be done, the movie will be over, and something else will be born and will begin. But it is not about the ending, it is about the journey itself. We just need to let go of some of the heaviness that we accumulate along the way. There is a story that when you die, you go up to the heavenly realm, and before you go in, you have to weigh your heart against a feather on the divine scales. If your heart is heavier than the feather, then you are sent back down for more learning. But if your heart is as light or lighter than the feather, then you are allowed to go in. It is a powerful story.

Can you be light-hearted at that level? With the world as it is, with all the chaos, crises, questions and worry about the future, with all the difficulties that we face, the divisions and the opinions, can you maintain light-heartedness? It does not mean that you make light of difficult things, it just means you carry light-heartedness in the core of your being.

If we want to be free, if we truly want to be free, we are going to have to drop some of this baggage that we are carrying – this person is wrong, that person is unenlightened, the other person is this or that. Being light-hearted means being empathic, and therefore able to see everything from the opposite viewpoint. This means that you can see your own viewpoint from its opposite with equal empathy, and so you can still hold your view, but you are going to hold it in a lighter way. You become aware of holding that view because it fits with your character, and the persona that you have in this life. In another life, you would have a different persona, yet you would have the same underlying consciousness.

We are going to have to expand way beyond these divisions that come into the world, whatever they are. Wherever our opinion settles, wherever our view lands, we have to hold it lightly. And that is where the whole of humanity is, in a sense, in the Uptight Buddha stage. And we have to hold this stage that we are in as lightly as possible and see that we are going to move through it. We are going to move progressively into transcendence. It is a journey, and the bliss and awakening in that journey are in how we get there, not when we get there, because every step is precious.

Being in the eternal present moment that the mystics continuously remind us of is the only thing that keeps us safe. It keeps us in the hub, the centre of the wheel, and then we do not get lost in the spokes. The spokes are all the different machinations, divisions, possibilities and viewpoints, with each spoke looking from a different place. It is wonderful to travel around some of those spokes and see through them, and yet we also need to be the one in the centre, in the hub which does not move and which never changes.

Wherever you are at in your being, in your body, your emotions, your relationships, your community, your job, your business, your purpose or lack of purpose, you can be an Uptight Buddha if you have to. It is all right. It is OK to be right where you are. You are needed there. But be there with awareness and contemplative mindfulness, and be there with love and acceptance of yourself. Then you can soften and yield into that presence, whatever comes up, whatever shape your life is currently taking. You will take a lot of pressure off your shoulders because you will stop wanting things to be different from the way they are. Although you may still have that evolutionary urge of wanting to improve and find more peaceful ways of being, it begins with us being right here in the present moment and really embracing it. What a beautiful, simple and timeless teaching that is.

THE SEED OF THE PRESENT

Consider that every single, present moment is a seed. Any project that you begin is contained in the first step, the first moment, and it is seeded with specific forces in that moment. Think about that in relation to DNA. Every cell of our body contains the map of the whole in its DNA. It is all in there. Every cell contains very specific instructions and forces that relate to that cell. Every little iota is a seed. It is the same with us and the same with nature. We are also a seed or an egg, and sometimes outside forces come and they rupture the wall and they shape us, but the blueprint underneath remains unchanged. Our psychology and ideology may change, but these are outside changes. Whatever happens on the outside, our essence never changes.

Every single moment contains a seed. Dharma, a Sanskrit term, which refers to the higher purpose of your soul, relates to this idea of the seed, and this too is encoded in every single moment. The insight of astrology is that the moment of your birth is also a seed, one that holds specific instructions and forces that will lead to the dharma being encoded in there, as a certain kind of life. Karma decides how that life will be shaped, but the seed is always there in the present moment. Karma is the seed opening up. Our every thought, act and word is thus a seed that we plant into every living moment.

If you think about the universe, the theory from physics is the idea that, at the beginning, the universe was compressed into a tiny space. That space was like a seed, and in that seed the entire universe was waiting, like an acorn with an oak tree hidden inside it. You can apply the same theory to time, because space and time are intricately linked, and if you are going to apply it to space, you have to apply it to time as well. So in the beginning, time was also condensed, and it is encoded in every single moment. Time is also fractal in the same way that space is fractal, and this is where the idea comes that time is geometric.

Every moment that we are alive, we are living in a moment that has grown from the past, and we are transmuting that seed of the past all the time. Whether it was traumatic or whether it was good, whatever it was, we are continually transmuting the seeds of the past that we have sown. So in every moment we have the opportunity to completely reset our future or to keep it as it is and maintain it through our behaviour patterns. Keeping to the same behaviour patterns invariably means continuing with the same future.

The great insight is that the present moment is the seed of the future. What a different world we would create if we really, truly understood that as a species, and if we really understood that our life does not just end at death but continues on and on, because our children and our grandchildren are seeds that are growing in turn, and a part of us is inside those seeds as well.

Really think about every seed that you sow in your life, every thought, word and deed, how you think of people, how you speak to people, and the decisions you make. Every single one of those things is a seed that you are planting in the universe, and every single one of those moments will sprout. Think of all those moments sprouting and then growing into trees. What have you sown? Is it a beautiful orchard full of fruit trees or is it lots of thorny brambles so tangled that you can't get through? Ask yourself: what am I sowing in my life in every present moment?

AWAKENING THROUGH LOVE

Here is something for lovers everywhere. We are all lovers. When you find a relationship that you know you can really work with, and in which you are both committed to a higher purpose, think of this story. A couple who loved each other deeply went to the Buddha and said, *'Lord, we love each other very much, but we are afraid of being separated by death.'* The Buddha replied, *'Keep following the Teachings, and following the love, and, together, if you are fortunate, those two things will allow you to be reborn in a single body as an enlightened one.'*

That is something that anyone can work towards. Whether you are with your loved one or looking for a loved one, hold that impulse at the core of your being. It is the highest impulse anyone can have in a relationship. The greatest service anyone can offer, to the world, to the cosmos, to humanity, is to make the step towards awakening. It does not matter what we do on the outside if we are not awake, because it will not have a true impact, although it may have an impact within the Maya, the world we live in.

What the world really needs is awakened beings, fully-realised beings, because in everything they do, a fully-realised being causes more people to awaken and become realised. This is the highest service anyone can offer in life. So create that seed, and plant it at the core of your relationship, or in your intentions for a relationship. It is pure selflessness to work together, to be reborn as two halves of a whole, in a single, glorious being, an awakened one. Can you imagine what kind of teachings would come through such a being?

That person would be able to teach true relationships, because of the incarnative crescendo that brought about their awakening, and through the loving of two halves becoming whole. It gives you the power to move through all the challenges, sufferings, difficulties and shadows that every relationship inevitably will bring up. With that as your compass, your North Star, you have the capacity to go all the way and further. And, then, when death does come, it will be revealed as simply a veil.

Occasionally, you will hear of a couple whose love is so great that when one dies the other doesn't experience their death in the expected sense, because the other person lives on fully in their heart. Behind that feeling can lie a selfless urge to serve the whole at the highest level possible. How wonderful that is.

COUNTENANCE DIVINE

When spring arrives and the weather starts picking up at home in the UK, I start slipping out of the house early to see the sunrise. One particular morning, I headed out for one of the first sunrises that I had caught that year. It was a beautiful morning and, as I was outside communing, some things came to me.

I had a very traditional, proper English education at a Christian school. It wasn't an overly Christian school, but we went to church on Sundays, and I would hear the words of the services, and recite them or sing them, without wondering really what they meant. Sometimes they come back to me though. And that morning, as I was out there in the dew, the sun glinting on the English meadows, with the divine essences and fragrances and sounds of the dawn, the birds, and the purity of it all, a word came back to me from the past – countenance – *the Countenance Divine*. I wasn't sure what it really meant, but that particular morning I saw it, and I experienced it. It was everywhere, surrounding everything like a shining cloak lighting up the world. If you look with eyes that see, you can see the Countenance Divine illuminating everything and you can see it even on the darkest days.

The phrase *'And does the Countenance Divine shine forth among those clouded hills,'* first appeared in William Blake's poem which became well-known as the hymn 'Jerusalem'. The Divine Countenance – it is wonderful. I used to associate those words with long, tedious Sunday services when I would rather have been somewhere else, but now it is completely different. Suddenly I see the Countenance everywhere, in everything.

I encourage you to go outside in the dawn. Go out in the first light and taste it. It doesn't matter if you are a little bit late. That morning I was a bit late and didn't catch the actual sunrise, but I was in it. I was bathed in it. It was exquisite. It is the ultimate spiritual practice to meet the sun at sunrise, to gaze at it, just with your peripheral vision if it is too bright. Take it into your bones, take it into your being and let the Countenance permeate your cells, your skeleton, all the layers of your being. You will find that the more you do it, the more it will resonate with the inner sun inside you, and it will completely change your day. So, go out and enjoy the Countenance – the Divine Countenance.

SWORD OF KNOWLEDGE, CHALICE OF WISDOM

It is very easy for someone like me to be misunderstood. I often am, particularly, by people who don't really have a spiritual impulse inside them, or at least not one that they have discovered yet, and then they look at what I am doing with the teachings of the Gene Keys and wonder, *'What is it? What is it founded on? It seems so obscure and non-scientific. I don't understand.'* This is the difference between knowledge and wisdom. The Gene Keys is about wisdom, which is very different from knowledge. The rest of the world, mostly the mainstream, is involved in knowledge. But I am in the business of wisdom.

Knowledge is like a sword, and wisdom is like a cup or chalice. The quest for knowledge is proactive and goes after what it wants. It uses the mind and dissects in order to understand things. It is endlessly exploring and endlessly hungry, wanting to understand things and put them together and make sense of them. It is the basis of science, of anything that is mental in nature, that involves understanding life and the things around us. We do not even think about it because we live in a knowledge society, on a knowledge planet.

Wisdom is very different because it does not go out there to cut things open to try to understand them. Wisdom comes through revelation, and revelation is something that opens up inside us. It involves waiting for things to be revealed from the inside out. Wisdom is something you imbibe. You drink of its chalice, and to drink of it, you have to really taste it. You have to listen to life, empathise, be silent, switch off the mind, and then wisdom comes through the whole being.

Wisdom arrives and arises and flowers within us as a revelation, which is very different from the seeking and acquiring of knowledge. Wisdom alights, and it does not have the same taste as knowledge because it is an ever-flowing source of nourishment for the soul. It does not answer all the questions which come from the questing part of the mind, but it does quieten all the noisy questions. That does not mean that they go away forever, but the questions are not as important as the wisdom, because wisdom brings balance. Balance is what we need in order to make clear decisions so that we can live a fulfilling life.

You can have wisdom without knowledge and you can have knowledge without wisdom, but it is best is to have a balance of both. There is a natural hierarchy, however, so if you put knowledge before wisdom, it is putting the cart before the horse and it will never work. You will not get anywhere until you put wisdom before knowledge. Wisdom will bypass the mind and go straight to the source of being, which is something more mysterious, and is more to do with silence. Wisdom thrives on mystery, and there is no end to the mystery of wisdom.

There is nothing in wisdom that wishes to solve the mystery because wisdom knows that the mystery cannot be solved by seeking with the mind. It can only be imbibed and embodied until we become part of the mystery, and when you *become* the mystery, everything in your life comes into balance. You then have lucidity in your mind because you are drawing from all elements of the cosmos and you are fed and nourished by something that goes far beyond knowledge.

Correct understanding of the two spheres of knowledge and wisdom (and how different they are) is really important.

When you look out in the world and you see people engaged only in the path of knowledge, you know that, somewhere deep within them, they are always going to be unhappy and unfulfilled. They may have moments of happiness like we all do, but until you can tap the source of wisdom, you can never slake the thirst that the mind has. You can never feel the engagement of that eternal spirit inside you, because wisdom is infinite, and knowledge cannot encompass infinity. It cannot possibly ever crack the chestnut of mystery that is infinity. It is not of the same dimension and so there is no way it can understand it. But it can penetrate some of the workings of the universe which can be of immense help for us as a species to help solve real-life problems, and all kinds of things in our societies that help us live healthier, happier lives.

Ultimately, until we come to the true source of wisdom inside us and tap the universal spirit of the eternal, it is all for nothing, because we are just rats in mazes, chasing our own tails and forever trying to solve problems that are rooted in a much deeper place inside us, in the Divine Feminine, in the chalice.

So it's best to have both – carry the sword of knowledge, but drink first from the chalice of wisdom, which is in your body, your being, your spirit, and is something beyond words. It is felt in the deep silence of the night and the silence between words, in between the dreams of this world, the hopes and wishes and yearnings that humans have. Underneath all of that lies wisdom. Contemplation is a technique and an art that shows you how to drink from the chalice of wisdom.

And then everything else comes into its own balance. Knowledge and wisdom – sword and chalice – carry them both with equal vigour, love and appreciation.

NOTHING TO DEFEND

Known to his followers as Maharaj Ji, Neem Karoli Baba was a Hindu guru and spiritual teacher who became internationally renowned in the 1960s. He died in 1973, and there are many stories told about him. In one story, one of his devotees was a scientist, and his best friend, who was also a scientist, was always teasing him saying, *'Why is such an intelligent man like you taken in by these guru frauds? With your scientific viewpoint I just can't believe it.'* And the devotee just said, *'Look, I don't try to convert you or anyone, so just leave it be.'* But his sceptical friend continued teasing him about it as he just could not understand.

Then one day, Neem Karoli Baba came to the city where the two friends lived, and as it happens he was holding a meeting nearby. The devotee went to see him, and his friend went along too, to see the 'fraud' for himself. He wanted to meet the man who had seemingly kidnapped the psyche of his great friend.

When they arrived at the meeting, Neem Karoli Baba said to the sceptical friend, *'Welcome. You forgot to wear your locket today. You must go and put it back on.'* The man was absolutely stunned. He turned to his friend, the devotee, and explained that the locket that Neem Karoli Baba was speaking of was given to him by the doctor who saved him twenty years ago when he had cancer. This doctor was a very special man, and he had told him to always wear the locket to remind him that he would always be well. He had indeed worn the locket every day of his life until that very day when it turned out that he had left it in the bathroom. This was the only time he had ever forgotten to put it on. That was his introduction to Neem Karoli Baba, and from that moment on he became his devotee too.

We all know someone like that man. People who are sceptical, cynical, defensive, overly scientific and overly materialistic, and they have forgotten a holistic view – which is understandable because of the nature of the world and how we are conditioned in this current age.

The point of this story is that such people are just an inch away from being awakened by something happening that reminds them that there is more. However, it is not your job to convert such people in any way, and my recommendation is not to put yourself in a position where you need to be in any way defensive towards people who are sceptical about your path. You simply don't go there, but say, *'This is my way and it's part of who I am.'* Don't preach it and don't try to convert anyone. Instead, go the opposite way and move into small talk.

This is the approach I take with people. Unless they directly ask me, I won't tell them what I really do, or who I am. They have really got to want to know. Even if I tell them that I have written a book about philosophy and spirituality, if they drop the subject I don't go any further. They have to really probe if they want to know more. They have to show that they are really interested. Then I open up, if they are willing to make the time and the space, which is rare in this day and age.

I recommend that you play hard to get like that, and do not feel in any way pressured around other people. Just enjoy their company, as one human to another. You could buy them a drink, or be generous in some way, and extend some humanity towards them. Just listen to them. Listen to their story without the need for them to hear yours. Then you will gain their trust, or not, but this is the approach I like. It makes your life simple.

I have some wonderful Jehovah's Witnesses who come to talk to me. Most people have had a Jehovah's witness come to their door at one time or another. I think they must be very lonely to keep going to the doors of strangers, but they feel that they have a message that they need to give to convert others. They are very gentle in their approach, but still they approach. I am not exactly a Christian, but I am a follower and devotee of Christ, as well as many other teachers. So I am always very open to the Jehovah's Witnesses visiting, and I talk to them a little bit and try not to scare them off too much.

They usually give me one of their pamphlets which sometimes contain great value, and I always skim through and have a read. This is a nice quote I found in one of them, from the Bible – Psalm 37:10, *Just a little while longer and the wicked will be no more. You will look at where they were, and they will not be there. But the meek will possess the earth and they will find exquisite delight in the abundance of peace.'*

WINGS OF LIBERATION

One morning, an amazing thing happened when I went out to see the sunrise. I saw the connection between the animal kingdom, nature, our outer world, and us, and the connection between the codes of the matrix of life and our inner world, our inner nature.

I was out walking in the meadows, where there are often many birds, and some seagulls came and started mewing and whirling around in the morning light. They often make a mewing sound in the mornings, and also a deep kind of laughing sound. I bowed in supplication to the sun, and started to walk home, when I noticed that one seagull was following me along the road. It flew with me all the way into the village, and I wondered why.

I seemed to be the only person up and about so early in the morning, so I walked into the car park by the local pub, which was quite a large, wide-open space, and I just stood there. The gull started swirling around me, making its mewing sound, and suddenly it dived towards me and came right at me. I felt the exhilaration of the moment as the bird swooped past me and carried on whirling, rising and falling and turning in the sky while I stood there, turning and following it. It flew up and came back, then it came around and dived again.

Every time it dived at me I could hear the whoosh of the wind through its feathers, the quiet of the early morning amplifying the sound. It was just me and the gull in a dance for about fifteen minutes. I was in a state of rapture.

I saw the connection between the outer and the inner, and the power of a symbol when we allow it to move deep within us. The cry of the gull is the rapture of liberation, cutting free from the Maya, the illusion, and ascending into the inner skies of consciousness. The seagull represents Liberation, the Siddhi of the 39th Gene Key. It is a vision of liberation, the great seabird soaring into the heavens, riding the thermals over the great oceans of life.

We can often allow the sounds that interrupt our lives to irritate us, and I could easily have felt that morning that I just wanted a nice quiet dawn. But if you let that sound in and allow it to percolate and be absorbed, then instead of being a sound that might irritate you, it can liberate you, giving you a rush, a feeling of awe, or a moment of transport. And it could be the same with any sound, though particularly the sound of a bird or an animal, because they are communicating with us from inside us. Every creature is a programming chip within the matrix of the illusion in which we live. We are all pieces of a code, and they are a piece of code within a piece of code.

There is a great dance here to enjoy the playfulness of the Tao, the unfurling of our evolution, our story and our mythology, as we live and move and have our being in this world.

ARCHETYPAL REALITY

When you hear the word 'archetype', you might wonder what it actually means. My view is that archetypes are a coalescence of the collective consciousness of humanity – of our thought patterns, our beliefs and our ideals. To begin to understand how archetypes have meaning in our lives, you could look at the diagram of the different subtle bodies and their corresponding planes that make up our 'Rainbow Body' – or aura.

Starting with the Physical or Etheric Body and moving outwards, we have the Astral or Emotional Body and the Astral Plane, the Mental Body and the Mental Plane, the Causal Body and the Causal Plane, and then further out, the Buddhic, the Atmic and the Monadic Bodies and their planes. Of these, the Causal Plane is the domain of archetypes, where thought and feeling become one as they are combined and transcended on the threshold of that plane. They lie beyond our feelings and desires, and beyond our mind, although they interpenetrate both the emotional and the mental bodies.

The world of thought – the mental body and its plane – lies just beyond the emotional body, which is reflected in the interconnection between the way you think and the way you feel. And, although thought is generally seen as a subtle vibration, there are both denser and subtler thought patterns within the field of thought. Each frequency has a grading within the layers, and each layer has a threshold between it and the next.

The Rainbow Body is explored more deeply within the set of teachings that I call the Corpus Christi (meaning literally the Body of Christ). It is the science of our higher reality, a key to the true underlying nature of all human beings and one of the journeys of the Gene Keys Synthesis. As we ascend in understanding through the subtle bodies and their planes, and the relationships of the different layers within the framework, our embodiment of the unified consciousness of all that is expands.

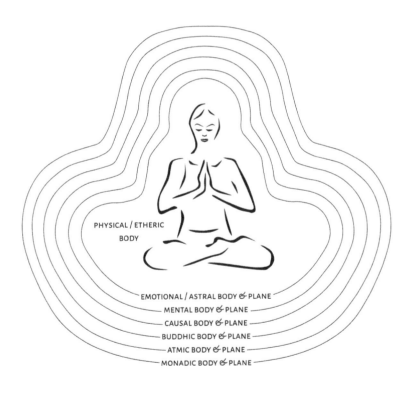

PHYSICAL / ETHERIC BODY

EMOTIONAL / ASTRAL BODY & PLANE
MENTAL BODY & PLANE
CAUSAL BODY & PLANE
BUDDHIC BODY & PLANE
ATMIC BODY & PLANE
MONADIC BODY & PLANE

THE RAINBOW BODY

An archetype can be a lens giving you a view into the holographic interdimensional cosmos. Here is an example. I was walking at dawn one morning when I saw two doves sitting together in the sunlight. It was beautiful, and on one level it was an archetype, because doves symbolise love and peace. Two doves sitting together in the first rays of sunlight could be seen as a classic archetype of love. But I could also look at those birds and see two living creatures that could be shot and dissected to see what they are made of. On the other hand, if I were looking through a poet's eyes, I might write about the doves representing a cosmic love between yin and yang.

The higher cultural forms, such as poetry, music and art, those highest forms of human aspiration, touch the threshold of the causal plane, and they download the archetype. But even the highest intellectual thought will not reach the causal plane, because there is a kind of veil here which the logical mind cannot penetrate.

To enter into the causal plane you have to let go of the mind. It involves a form of higher thinking, imbued with knowing, so it is a very high state of consciousness. It can be accessed through deep insights, epiphanies and breakthroughs. This is how the causal plane comes into human consciousness, through sudden rushes of knowing that enter into our physical, emotional and mental bodies in the 'Aah' moments when you suddenly know the truth of something – although they may, at some level, feel more akin to memories.

It was Jung who first used the term 'archetype' and who coined the phrase 'shadow archetypes', and he was one of the great exponents of the archetype. Other great thinkers have explored archetypes, right back to Plato, but Jung in particular saw them as coming from the collective consciousness.

They are fundamental truths encoded through the different lenses that humans have picked up. There is a whole spectrum of archetypes which interlock, and they are not all pretty.

The entertainment and publishing industries are in the business of decoding and translating archetypes into films and books. For example, in the horror genre – what is a vampire? Where has this figure come from? It is an archetype of a certain behaviour or a certain pattern. The vampire can be seen as a shadow archetype, and it represents something that perhaps our mind cannot fully grasp, although we might experience vampire-like behaviour in others. We might even exhibit it ourselves, when we latch on to something and won't let go, and keep trying to 'suck the blood' out of it, which is a selfish kind of behaviour in that sense.

Note that experiencing a shadow archetype on the causal plane does not mean that you will identify with it, whereas you will if you view it from the emotional, the astral plane. Imagine, for example, that you are sleeping, and you are in your astral body, dreaming about a vampire. On the astral plane, you believe that you are separate from the vampire and that it is coming to get you. On the causal plane, however, you know that the vampire is an archetype. It is a fractal aspect of truth, and you cannot distinguish it from a heightened aspect of truth. You would not discriminate between the archetype of love as seen in the two doves and the archetype of the vampire because they are both made of light, because at their core they are both experiences of the collective consciousness.

So seeing things from the causal plane is a real quantum leap for humans, because it means we no longer identify with the dramas of the world. For instance, there are people who believe that there are men in black, or some kind of dark cabal, controlling the world, trying to take away our freedom and our power, and there might be some truth in that. But seen from the causal plane, such conspiracies are not identified with, because you realise that they are all facets of the Maya, the illusory drama, the theatre that we are all players in. Once you realise that, you can still enjoy the good versus evil game because we happen to be in one, but you don't get caught in it.

Seeing things from this higher plane means that you are no longer so attached to your own frame of reference, and you begin to appreciate the true patterns of life and nature. Archetypes are everywhere. Once we begin to decode them, we realise that we are enmeshed in them, and many of us are lost in them.

Now, you might ask, *'How can I get to the causal plane?'* The answer is through deep contemplation, and you have to be really courageous because you are contemplating something about yourself – the way that you are seeing something, or any discomfort you may be experiencing. You have to take a long, honest look at yourself, and the beauty is that if you go into deep contemplation or meditation for periods of time, you will begin to see things clearly and understand. The art of contemplation is key and is something that I really recommend learning. It is quite simple, and when we start to create pauses in our day and in our life, we are opening up the space for contemplation and for the insights to drop in.

There may be some great mystery in your life that you don't understand – a relationship, your health, or anything that you want to get to the bottom of, or it could be that you had a significant dream that you don't understand. Whatever it is, you contemplate it and you do not give up. You contemplate it by filtering it with your mind and your feelings, and you go on contemplating it until the penny drops and you have an insight. Because, over a period of time, if you stay relaxed, the causal plane will open up and the insight will come, almost certainly, at the oddest or most unexpected time. It might be triggered by something that someone says, by an event or a dream.

The insight drops in, the skies open and you realise that you have gained yourself a little bit of freedom. A lot of freedom, actually, because you are no longer being possessed by the archetype. Because you are now seeing that, whatever the archetype is, and even if it appears to be sinister, it is made of light. You do not discriminate between good and bad archetypes, and therefore you can exist in a deep state of trust. Our lives are filled with archetypes that can be decoded.

Visual images of archetypes start to form on the causal plane, but they are not just visual – they are impregnated with feeling, texture, colour, shape and memory – they are multidimensional. So archetypes are multidimensional facets of consciousness and mystery. And the more that you can decode inside your being, the more you will rise towards the Buddhic Plane, and you realise that there is light behind everything and that everything can be reduced to light. You cannot see that from the mental plane, because there your thoughts can be quite interdimensional and advanced. You might have a thought about the unity of consciousness, for example, but the actual experience of it could be very different. On the causal plane, however, you experience it and remember it because you inhabit it not just through intellectual understanding, but beyond that in knowing. The knowing is beyond both intellectual understanding and feeling, but it contains both.

The Buddhic Plane, which lies just beyond the Causal Plane, does not deal in archetypes. Images and archetype are not formed there. So, when the Buddhic Plane starts to come through, you no longer need to think about the archetypes, and as your contemplation expands, you begin to experience those higher states of absorption where you are filled with light and love. It is just pure light, undifferentiated, coming through the heart centre, and it is all about experiencing feelings of exalted ecstasy and cosmic love.

The magic of the art of contemplation leads us through insights, epiphanies and breakthroughs into the field of merging, where we realise that, even though everything differentiates as it comes down into the form and into our mind, there are higher levels in which things are undifferentiated while unified in diversity. That is the real insight. We don't just merge into a soup. We actually experience the merging as it is occurring, but we also experience the differentiation as it comes right down into our life and our mind. It is an epic journey.

THE BODY OF GLORY

Omraam Mikhaël Aïvanhov was a great master from Bulgaria who has had a deep influence on me. One of his teachings was on the concept of the Body of Glory, about which he said:

'God dwells in our Body of Glory. The New Testament tells us that we possess an incorruptible body of pure light, which we call the Body of Glory. In the very distant past, this body enabled human beings to travel through space and to see and understand the whole of creation. But as they became more and more deeply immersed in the denser layers of matter, humans neglected their Body of Glory until it became incapable of manifesting itself. And now we have to reverse this movement and nourish and care for it so that it can be restored to its former function.

It is thanks to our Body of Glory, after all, that we shall live eternally, and recapture the powers that were ours in the past. All the forces of creation are at the disposal of those who nourish their Body of Glory, until it attains its full stature, for it is in this glorious body, not in our physical body, that God dwells.'

The Body of Glory or the 'Rainbow Body' is the higher harmonic body of our true being. We used to inhabit it, and we still do at some level, but in this phase of our evolution, we have forgotten it. Yet you can nourish the Body of Glory through grasping moments of awe, moments of transport.

Every time you have a transcendent moment or an epiphany, your Body of Glory is flooded with light and it expands. As we keep on experiencing those moments, the Body of Glory will keep growing through the realisation of the beauty of life, of all that is best and that is highest. This is why you have to look for those higher things and grasp them. If you keep reading and listening to books and teachings that nourish you, and if you keep opening up to moments of awe, you will keep plugging yourself back into the Body of Glory.

When you experience one of those moments, those rushes, your Body of Glory responds and grows, and you will feel a flood in your Rainbow Body as you are reminded of your infinite and eternal nature.

Once we have the abilities and the power of creation that Omraam Mikhaël Aïvanhov spoke of, which we will again one day, everything we think will instantly occur. But just imagine if we had that now, it would be chaos! Because first we have to purify all our karma so that every thought that comes into us is pure. They are not thoughts that come from us, but thoughts that we tune into that come through us. That is why thought can be so powerful.

The Body of Glory can be reinvigorated through purified thought, by nourishing it with the purest and most luminous elements. Just be careful to filter out impurities of thought and feeling. And when you experience a difficult emotion, check in to see what effect that might have on your Body of Glory. It won't negatively affect it, but you won't be nourishing it, and you will be feeding the shadow body instead.

There is a choice of which body you are going to feed through your state of mind. Through the law of affinity, through your thoughts, your feelings and your desires, you draw the surrounding elements and emanations into your aura, and into your Body of Glory. That is how you can capture particles of pure, eternal, incorruptible matter.

When we capture just one of those particles, through a moment of transport or transcendence, there is a little atomic explosion through our Body of Glory. We may experience that as an epiphany, an insight or as a moment of elation. It is during those moments that the Body of Glory sends pulses of light through us.

So we have to keep our connection all the time, as much as we can, to that higher body – the Body of Glory.

MANJUSHRI'S SWORD

I have a beautiful, 120-year-old Tibetan painting called a *thangka*. It was given to me by a friend, and it depicts the Bodhisattva Manjushri, a male Buddha emanation, wielding a flaming sword. This type of icon, of a being holding a flaming sword, sometimes two-edged, is quite common. Icons of this kind are fascinating to anthropologists for their symbolic meanings, and they can be very powerful when we understand their real meaning. We can then bring their guidance and wisdom into our everyday life because their purpose is to assist us in transcending time, thoughts and ideas.

For me, the sword that Manjushri is wielding represents the cutting power of the higher mind, of clarity and honesty – self-honesty. The sheen on the steel of the blade represents that honesty, the ability to look within yourself and see truth, to see who you are, what you are and what you have done, with clarity and with valour. This is about seeing both the good and the bad, which is actually the foundation of the higher path towards wisdom and awakening. Without this foundation, without the sense of deep stability that comes from that level of courage of looking at yourself, you don't have the foundation to be able to continue up the ladder, to continue to expand.

Without honesty, you endanger yourself, because if you open yourself up to higher currents and yet don't see who you are and what you are, then you are in danger of bringing crisis upon yourself. You may be bringing a deep destabilisation into your life, and, basically frying a circuit somewhere, which is a nice way of saying 'going a little bit crazy'.

This combination of being on a spiritual path and yet being unable to be honest with oneself is dangerous. It is precisely when the universe delivers us a cut from Manjushri's sword.

The sword is two-edged because it cuts both the past and the future. One side cuts the past by severing our attachments to who we think we are, because of who we have been, the things we have done, both positive and negative, as well as the difficulties that we often have in our childhood. We all collect patterns and programs from our peers when we are young, which is part of our ancestral wounding. Manjushri's sword helps us to cut away the ties that connect us to these patterns, paradigms and programs that keep us set on a victim course, and which keep manifesting certain difficulties and dramas in our lives.

When you are able to cut the past, you also take ownership of it. It doesn't mean that you jettison the past, but that you celebrate it as much as you can, to understand that it is a part of who you are. It has brought you where you are now, whether that is good or bad according to your mind. We are the summation of all that we have done, the good and the bad, and we have to come to terms with all of that inside ourselves. Manjushri's sword is very good at helping us to acknowledge it all without being weighed down by the heavy burden of guilt or shame.

The other side of the sword cuts the future, our dreams, our fantasies, our hopes and sometimes our delusions of what we may become and where we see ourselves going. We need to be able to sever those attachments cleanly because we don't know what is going to happen in the future, unless you are one of the gifted ones who can see that, which is very rare.

The moment a wish is transferred into the Mental Plane it becomes an image or a paradigm of something that we would like to happen. We want to have it and to make it come about. We see our life going towards that goal, and we plan the details of how we might like it to look. It is natural for the mind to do that, but of course it is all just in the air and we don't know whether any of it will occur. Even if intuitively we feel it will, we do not know. But what we do know are the deepest wishes of our soul, and they are something that we can trust and rely on.

We can feel the integrity of our heart's wishes, our soul's yearning for something higher, something greater, some sense of wholeness that we can rely on, but everything else is uncertain. Manjushri's sword brings us back to the purity of our uncertainty, without it being destabilising, because that honest uncertainty is actually very pure.

Using Manjushri's sword to cut the past and the future is done simply by looking at yourself with a piercing honesty. You need to look at all that you are, into the dark crevices of your mind, your memory and your heart, and also under any stones that you find. See the good and the bad and weigh it all with equanimity and without judgment. Then you will see what you are and you can approach the divide, or the higher, greater world from a place of truth.

The codes of the Gene Keys represent the illusion, the Maya which we inhabit, and they are not just a set of ideas, because they are, in a sense, alive, and they are powerful when you start examining them and applying their wisdom in your own life.

You will see that the dramas that we experience, the *lilas*, games and dances that are played out in our day-to-day lives, are giving us feedback. Because what is inside us will manifest outwardly, and so the experience of a *lila* or drama will help us to see more clearly what we are working out inside us.

We then have to use our discernment to work out what that aspect is offering us and teaching us.

What is your life showing you about you right now? Is it showing you something that you haven't fully admitted about yourself? That is a really positive thing to discover underneath one of those stones inside our nature.

I encourage you to be super-clear inside yourself about who you are, what you have done and any delusions you may be holding, or any expectations you may have, and any guilt that you are carrying. None of it is wrong, so just see it for what it is, and from there, from that place of truth, you can progress in a clear way. Life will offer you that progression and teach you, and the dharma will fuel your progress. You need Manjushri's sword to cut away the delusions.

The Vedas give us the image of the Maya, the illusion in which we live, that we believe is real – life out here in the phenomenal world – as a net. They call it Indra's Net and it is said that we are caught in it. And the great thing about that is that if you are caught in a net, but you have a sword, you can cut the net and free yourself. You do not have to cut every single knot of the net. You have to cut only three or four that happen to be next to each other, and then you can slip through into liberation.

Consider the junctions that life brings you through the dramas and the *lilas* of your outside life. What are they showing you? They are pointing you towards something very specific. If you can listen to what they are teaching you, you can cut those knots in the net and then something will open inside you. Then you will be presented with another one and you can cut that one too. It takes what the Buddhists term 'skilful means', the ability to use the sword to gently cut away the dross, the places where we are dishonest with ourselves, the places of denial.

It is important to realise here that a sword is a sword, and it needs to be sharp. You can use it gently, but you still have to cut, and it is you that you are cutting – the parts of your illusion. So wield it gently, but also wield it carefully and decisively, with discernment. Have the courage to really look at yourself with candid and penetrating clarity, with brutal honesty and with deep valour. This is the foundation of self-compassion, to be able to see oneself clearly taking in everything that you are, the light and the dark, without judgement. Take heart and wield Manjushri's sword gently and with grace.

BEHIND THE VEIL

Every now and then, once you have been working in a committed way with the Gene Keys, perhaps over some years, you will have an epiphany, which can be an extraordinary experience. Epiphanies have three stages: the insight, the breakthrough and the epiphany itself. The insight comes from a subtle opening up of the Mental Plane.

The breakthrough is an emotional rush, a heart-opening experience through the emotional frequency of the Buddhic Plane. And the epiphany is an acausal event that happens outside space and time. It is an event triggered by grace. The only thing that may create an epiphany event is deep, deep patience, and that patience has to be coupled with love and other higher qualities. But every now and then they happen, and when they do it is deep inside the cellular DNA. Epiphanies open up memories, pathways and our core structure, and they allow us to see things and remember things that are fundamental to reality, or to what we call reality.

I experience epiphanies sporadically, not so often, maybe once a year or every few years. One epiphany, which I cannot fully explain, except just one aspect of it, was when I found myself marvelling at the utter beauty of nature in the midst of the epiphany. These words came to me, *'It's a very convincing imitation of reality – nature, everything, this beauty. It's a very convincing imitation of reality.'* Think about that when you look at the trees, the rocks, the sky, your house, your family, your friends, your own hands. It is a very convincing imitation of reality. Let those words sink into your soul. They came from deep within the structure of my DNA. I did not say them. They were spoken as an epiphany.

Everything around us is an illusion. We have heard this, but to know it, to remember it, even for a short space of time, is an extraordinary thing. We live in a matrix, as in the film 'The Matrix'. Other than what happens when the protagonist, Neo, wakes up, the film has things exactly right. We live in a matrix that is governed by binary coding and numbers. Everything is coded in a program and a sub-program. Your body is a program, and your mind too. Everything is programmed. Your house, the furniture around you, the trees outside, the feeling of the earth under your feet as you walk, it is all programmed. None of it is real in that sense. It feels real. It feels convincing that there is an in-here, and an out-there, but, actually, everything you see is a representation of your inner core. Everything. It is just like a dream. Everything is symbolic. Every event that occurs to you, every challenge you are moving through, is a symbol. It is a myth that you are moving through.

Then the inner breakthrough occurs around that, when suddenly something happens and you start to take it less seriously, and a detachment arises in you. It is a lot to take in, that we are in a programmed cosmos, that there is a veil over our eyes. The beauty of it is that we are actors in a theatre, so watch it and enjoy it as much as you can. Even pain at a certain level can be watched, and perhaps not enjoyed, but it can be appreciated as a transformative process within the Maya, within the illusional world.

We are held by the magnetic forces of these dimensions, our planes of existence, but every now and again we catch glimpses through the veil. Our spiritual practice, our *sadhana*, can provide us, through our endocrine system, with cracks that open up within the Maya, that allow our body and being to access these insights and epiphanies that give us a glimpse of the illusion.

If you think about these things as you go about your day, don't let them disturb you. If you continue to travel with the Gene Keys, you will see that the codes of the Gene Keys are designed to begin to break open the Maya that we live in and allow us to see further into the mystery, and see aspects of the illusion beginning to break down.

The Gene Keys are the exact codes of the matrix, so as you work with them, you are deprogramming the matrix, especially the Shadows. You transform the Shadows into the Gifts, and, as this happens, your theatre changes. It starts being more fun, for one thing, but also more light comes into the matrix. Your narrative shifts to become positive, instead of being a negative tale of suffering. Then as the Gifts begin to transform into the Siddhis, the whole matrix begins to shudder and shimmer, and you begin to see the cracks and the glimpses of light from behind the veil, which is all part of the process of breaking open the Maya.

The stage is set, the curtain is up... I wish you well in your theatre!

THE LIFE OF WAKEFULNESS

What does it mean to be wakeful? Béla Hamvas, a wonderful Hungarian sage, offers this contemplation:

'The spirit does not have qualities, because only the spirit exists – it is the only substance. But the spirit is not active. It does not create. It does not move. It does not change. But it is wakeful. That is why the old ones said that the measure of the human spirit's life is wakefulness.

Wakefulness does not direct towards action. Wakefulness is not characteristic of thinking or reflection. It is not the sharpness of the senses, it is not the tense alertness of the powers. It is not intelligence. Thus, wakefulness reveals itself in a world that is not spirit, but merely the mirage of the spirit.

Wakefulness is not action, is not consciousness, is not comprehension, is not seeing, is not knowing. Thus, wakefulness reveals itself only in the secondary world, the lower world. It is impotent attraction to all that is spirit. It is soft devotion to all that is spirit. It is irresistible connecting to all that is spirit.

The real wakefulness is love. This is why the ancient ones said that the great and good, beautiful human life is not the one that is active, vast, powerful, scientific, prosperous, famous, glorious – but the one that is wakeful.

Wakefulness is not knowledge, not power, not strength, not activeness – but love.'

I love what Hamvas says. It is something eternal and elusive, something indefinable. He says that the spirit does not have qualities, but you can't really say that. The only thing you could say about it, in the mirage world in which we live, is that it has a quality of wakefulness, and the closest we can come to this wakefulness, as an approximation, is in lovingness, devotion and softness.

The softness is a tint through which spirit sees everything. It softens and rounds hard edges, and it connects, binds and unifies, but it has no power of its own. It is just the connectiveness of life at work. It can be drowsy in some people, and it can be dormant in others, and when you see it like that, it is often someone living a hard life, someone suffering, someone determined, and perhaps someone the ego might find impressive. But the soft life, the life of the water mind, is a hidden life. That is the life of wakefulness, that is the life of the spirit – it is often an invisible life.

CHAPTER 2

ALCHEMY

*Our lives are punctuated by transformational
experiences and breakthroughs. They may be
personal, within a relationship or a community,
or in relation to humanity and the world.*

*The alchemy is in the transformation of old thought
patterns or fixed viewpoints that we can't let go of,
or aspects of the shadows that we carry within us.
Through contemplation and awareness they can be
unlocked, transformed and released, and then we
can exist in a higher state of harmony and grace.*

THE EMBER OF FAITH

Sometimes, when we close our eyes and go inside, we find great darkness. We find despair, numbness, pain, fear, distraction, anxiety. All those and many other similar states are inside us, and they are there to be transformed. One day they will all have to be transformed. We have to do it, and we have no choice in that. If you don't do it now, you will have to do it later and, either way, it requires faith.

Faith is a word that has many levels and layers. It does not appear as a Siddhi, a Gift or a Shadow in the Gene Keys, but it is essential for the transformation of our shadows. Because when you meet the shadow it can feel overwhelming, and you need faith in order even to begin the work of transformation. Sometimes, when in contemplation, all you experience is the shadow, and you can't feel the light. Some part of you knows the light is there, but you can't find your way to it because you are in a tunnel.

We encounter and move through many tunnels throughout our journey. Different things can trigger a tunnel experience and it can happen at any time. You could just wake up in the morning and find yourself in one. Then you need the faith that there is a light at the end of it. It is vital to have that faith. It is the memory that you have done this before and that the shadow frequency that you are moving through cannot overwhelm you.

The ember of that faith is like a tiny light inside your heart. So when you are in a tunnel, go right to the core of your being, go into your heart of hearts and find that glowing ember in the darkness. When you have found it, and you always will, rest in it, settle into it and wrap your awareness around it. Just as you would use an ember to start a fire, gently blow on it and bring it alive. Nurture it and give all your attention, not to the darkness, but to the ember.

Given time, you will begin to glow and radiate warmth and light from inside you. That light is the light of your faith, radiating from that little ember, and it will glow brighter, and it will grow stronger. It will begin to disperse the darkness and soon you will begin to feel lighter inside.

That is our work. Some days it may seem overwhelming, but faith is doing it every day, over and over, turning the lens of your contemplation inwards and seeing what needs to be done. Ask yourself, *'What is my work today?'* And then give your attention to that and trust in it. Your faith will glow, and it will grow each day, because it is nothing more than the memory of the light that you truly are – not the darkness, but the light.

Give your attention to that ember. Do it over and over again, and you will find yourself moving in fewer and fewer tunnels, and over time the light will glow brighter and brighter.

GENTLING THE SHADOW

One morning, I woke up at 4am feeling a heaviness inside me. I sat up in bed and considered what to do. Taking my awareness inside myself, I went within, and I could feel the heaviness and a pain deep down in my belly. It was a shadow, a world shadow, my shadow, it didn't matter which, it was just a shadow, just pain, just suffering. But I gave it my attention. It had woken me up, after all. So I allowed my mind to explore it and to drift off, to drift back, drift off and drift back again, as the mind does, thinking of the things of the world.

These moments are a journey, like being in a boat on the ocean. The weather changes and the boat moves up and down. Suddenly you remember one of your great teachers, and there is a swell and you remember the light. You bring the light in, then you forget again and your contemplation dips. You drift. Something else comes in. You come back again. Eventually the mind drifts back to the subject on which it hadn't wanted to spend too much time. It is all a dance with the shadow, the discomfort. You just have to wrap your awareness around it and be with it. Whatever it is, just sit with it. Be forgiving and be gentle. Keep bringing the mind back, and bringing your awareness back.

There is nothing to fear, for it is just some discomfort, just some world shadow that has come up in the night. It could be something that has come up from your ancestral line so that you can process it and transmute it. It could be many things, but whatever it is, there is some grace in that shadow. It is a little treasure box. We have to give ourselves to it and explore it as best we can. If we manage to stay with it, we will carry it with us through the day and discover some of the light inside, and maybe, in some way, we will see it reflected in our day.

Contemplating the shadow means going within and being with the pain there. It may not be a great, clenching pain, but it is there and you just have to be with it. So be with it softly. Allow it time and space to reveal what it is and what it wants you to hear. Light a candle, say a prayer. Do something to ignite the Siddhi inside you, to bring counterbalance to that suffering. It is a simple teaching and a beautiful practice.

TRANSFORMING THE SHADOW

We all know suffering in varying degrees. All human beings suffer, and the shadow refers to those aspects of our nature that cause us to suffer. Transforming the shadow is the essence of the Gene Keys, and it is applicable and of use to all human beings.

The shadow can be many things. It can be repressed aspects of our nature that lie deep in our unconscious that we do not accept about ourselves, or it may be that they get vented regularly but still feel uncomfortable. It could be rage. It could be fear. It could be any number of difficult emotions that are blocked up inside us and causing us difficulty.

The shadow is rooted in fear, and at the deepest level, it is rooted in the fear of death. If you think that you are not afraid of death, try looking again into that fear, deeply. The fear of annihilation, the fear that you may no longer exist, the fear of dying, of pain, of loss are all connected to the fear of death. The shadow is all of that and much more. It is everything that is unprocessed, everything about ourselves that we don't like, that we don't feel comfortable about, and it is the very reason that we suffer in life.

The Gene Keys is a system and a modality for embracing the shadow, for getting to know it and unlocking its higher purpose and higher meaning. The Gene Keys show us our shadow patterns, and what is hidden inside them, so when you look at a shadow, you can crack it open and find the treasure hidden within. The very essence of the Gene Keys is 'Every Shadow contains a Gift'. It is a one-liner that I often use and it is not just a handy catchphrase. It is quite possibly the greatest truth humanity could ever discover.

We all have deep shadow patterns. Whether they are connected with our health, emotions, loved ones or our relationships, we all have those things in our life that are uncomfortable and can be deeply disturbing. How we grow the shadow out, transform it and shape it into the beautiful thing inside itself is the work, the alchemy. It is a long labour for all of us because we come with baggage that we carry with us, our karma, and it is there to be transformed. We have to face it and reshape it in order to make the most of our lives, because we carry it forward with us.

The process begins with acceptance, which sounds like such a simple thing, and yet it is subtle, deep and challenging. To start with, you have to look at what the pattern is. *What is this pattern inside me that is causing me this suffering, this pain?*

The Gene Keys give us a mirror, one with a very soft sheen, to look into our suffering. So when we have the courage, we can hold the mirror up and look our suffering in the face and see it for what it is. Then we can begin to feel differently about ourselves and about others, because the softness in the mirror is self-compassion and all that is best inside us: virtue, patience, tenderness, forgiveness, hope and many other beautiful qualities.

Through mindfulness, contemplation and meditation, you can get to a place where you can see the pattern, and see it without any agenda, without your fears, without even your hopes that it will go. Close your eyes now. Feel it in your body. It has a place. It has a story, but you do not need to worry about the story for now. Just allow the pattern as it is. Allowing is the first step towards acceptance.

The patterns have physical, emotional and mental components, as well as spiritual components that are hiding in the background. The patterns are grounded in our physical bodies, but they are also very emotional. So we have to be gentle with ourselves and look after our body, and try to eat and sleep well, even though the pattern itself may prevent that in the beginning. As we work with the pattern and become more familiar with it, we become softer in our approach towards ourselves and we learn to look differently at the shadow. Then many things in our biochemistry will start to change.

We all carry memories of difficult things inside us. Whatever kind of torment it may be, whether it is grief, rage or ancestral anguish that is not even of this life, there is also a deeper reason for everything, and you need to find that reason, that sense of a higher purpose. You do not have to understand it, but you have to let that glint of light in, because with that sense of higher purpose, your life one day could look very different. So, even right at the start, allow for the possibility that the pattern could change, that it could mutate and be transformed. There is a little pinprick of light and a hope that it can get better. It all depends on how you see it, and the core of that is *allowing*, which you need in order to be able to achieve acceptance.

So keep allowing the pattern, and looking honestly and softly at it for what it is. And forgive yourself when you wobble or lose yourself in that suffering or become overwhelmed by it. I know from my own experience that it is neither an easy nor a quick process. But it does get softer over time and the pain gets less as the body mutates, then the emotions become calmer and quieter and the mind becomes clearer. It will take time, though. The technique of contemplation allows you to look at the shadows in a kinder, softer light, and to look at yourself and others in a kinder, softer light.

So enter into this field of contemplation and locate the shadow, disabling it with your mind first. See how the mind controls it. Then begin to unravel it and you will realise its higher purpose. The Gene Keys and our community provide you with the resources to do this, as well as ways of going deeper into these processes. You can also find help and support from people who are on the same journey. These are people who sometimes share the gifts of their wonderful stories and advice, and those who have gone deeply into the transmission and the wisdom, and can thus offer their guidance and love as you move through the difficult areas in your life.

The Gene Keys teachings are full of resources, all created for the purpose of softening into these shadows and then transforming them, and it is also full of reminders for you to be gentle with yourself in this process.

The Gene Keys community is also here to help you. Whoever you are, whatever you bring, know that this may not be the only answer to your problems, but it certainly will address the core issue. A core statement of the Buddha is 'All life is suffering', and the core statement of the Gene Keys is 'Every Shadow contains a Gift', which is actually a distillation of the teachings of the Buddha and other great teachers as well.

Learning to allow, accept and embrace the shadow, and then watching it transform and your life along with it can be a very deep and lengthy process. But it is a way to experience considerable change in how your life operates and to discover something extraordinary inside yourself, something creative and dynamic that possibly you have always known was there. It is a unique journey for each person, but it is a journey that can be taken together. Ultimately we are here to find a pathway towards love. I hope your journey is deeply fulfilling.

TRUST IN TRUST

At the deepest level, almost every issue confronting humanity is an issue of trust. If you consider the things in your life that make you feel uncomfortable, it is very likely that you don't fully trust them. If you did, they wouldn't make you feel so uncomfortable. You may still suffer, but there wouldn't be an unease in you around them.

Trust doesn't appear as a Siddhi of the Gene Keys, but it underlies them all. We have to trust in the Siddhis, trust in the Shadows, and trust that the Shadows will reveal the Gifts. Trust is the answer. Trust everything. That is our learning. That is what we are here for. That is the single message of the Gene Keys, to remind us to trust everything. That means that when you find a lump somewhere in your body, trust that it is there for a reason. It is there to tell you something. If you get ill, trust the illness. It is telling you something, even perhaps that it is your time, in which case, trust the timing of your departure. Trust.

Even when looking at the terrible things in the world, trust them. I don't talk a lot about politics. I am not a political thinker, but I look at the things that happen in the world and I sense that underneath them is a sense of deep trust that all will be well. All is well. I trust that.

Everything is just the working out of what the ancients called the Tao – how to exist in harmony with the universe. Trust the Tao, the way, the path, the natural order of things. Trust in dharma, and its teaching, that everything is just playing itself out perfectly.

There is a danger, however, in saying that everything is perfect, because everything is very far from perfect from the human viewpoint, and this can lead to misunderstandings. For example, when you see someone suffering terribly, there is nothing perfect about that, it seems, yet at a deep level there is. There is a deep teaching in that person's suffering, for them and for everyone else around them. That is what we have to trust underneath. We don't have to like it, but we have to trust it. So if you find yourself feeling critical of something or someone, consider what it is about that person that makes you uncomfortable, and trust that thing, and trust the teaching that it is bringing to you.

Imagine yourself trusting everything, every second. That is awakening. That is self-realisation. That is absolute trust, absolute surrender. It is a subtle thing that can be misunderstood. Does it mean we don't have to do anything? Of course not. If someone comes at you with something negative, does that mean you don't do anything? Of course not. You have to trust in your response, trust in what comes up naturally for you, and trust in the teaching that comes out of that. If you react angrily, you will learn something from it, and that is to be trusted. Maybe the next time you will not react so strongly, as the trust in the teaching will have taught you something.

Trust is a cellular experience and a cellular knowing. It is a deep relaxation in the cells of the body. You can trust something mentally, and you can even trust it emotionally. But to experience it in the body is the deepest kind of trust. So, trust in the coming and going of humans, and the coming and going of our dramas, and the changing shapes of the weather, both internal and external.

Trust in the ridiculous dramas of the global stage, and the sometimes hilarious players – hilarious in the sense that they are like Shakespearean characters acting out their plays, which of course we participate in too, both as players and as audience.

This contemplation of trust, deep, cellular trust, is something to take into your life. Contemplate the places where you trust, and the places where you don't. It is all a learning. We are here on this planet for education. We are not here necessarily to enjoy heaven on earth, although we all have moments of that. Unless we are one of those rare people who have made that transition into pure trust, then most of our life is education. We are here to learn, and we learn in trust. That is the bottom line.

SPOILING THE MOMENT

Omraam Mikhaël Aïvanhov, a Bulgarian master, spoke of an aspect of our higher consciousness which he called the 'Body of Glory', which is taken from a mystical Christian understanding. Your Body of Glory is the highest expression of your being expressed as a field of light, your higher self, in a way, and it exists in dimensions other than this one. It is a secret, intangible thing, and not something you can show to anybody. It is something you can sense, and it can be sensed in other people too.

This body of light is something that we can grow, and it may grow in size, in intensity and in beauty throughout all our lives. One of the ways in which we can grow this body is through powerful expressions of awe in the present moment, by being utterly saturated by it and its beauty, and by allowing it to fill us and flood us. When those moments happen, our Body of Glory gets an influx of light from the beauty of all those moments, and so it grows. The more of those moments we create for ourselves, the more our Body of Glory expands around us and through us, and sends out impulses of good fortune, love and service in all directions.

There is now, a modern dilemma of giving away the beauty of the moment through our obsession with documenting it and posting it online. So, consider, the next time you are going to capture the moment or take a picture of yourself doing something wonderful to post on social media, that sharing these moments can become habitual. That is not to say that it can't be a wonderful thing, as it is a part of the natural sharing of our essence with each other, which can be beautiful.

So it is not that I am totally against such things, but I caution not to let it become the obsession that it can for many of us because then we can lose the golden secrecy of that beautiful, pregnant moment that we are experiencing. It could be that we are out in nature or that we make something beautiful, and immediately we want to photograph it and put it online to share. But some things are best not shared, and you might want to consider keeping them as secret moments for yourself, for your Body of Glory, for your soul. How precious, powerful and beautiful that is.

The irony is that the more we keep those moments of awe for ourselves, the more we build up a self-assurance that then transforms any anxieties that we may have about our sense of self. When we grab the camera to document the moment, it is often due to a lack of self-assurance or a lack of that sense of preciousness. We immediately want to give the moment away, and we give it away too cheaply, instead of drawing its sustenance and its nourishment deep into our souls and letting it live there.

So when you are out in the world, you could think about finding the balance between holding those precious moments for yourself and only sharing some of them, just the ones that feel truly appropriate.

THOUGHT WEATHER

I often think that thought is like the world weather. It can be a high-pressure, high-frequency system that pushes all the clouds away, or it could be a low-pressure, low-frequency system, which puts pressure on you inwardly and attracts the clouds.

Thought can transcend – it can open up and connect people, pathways, relationships and creativity. Yet we unconsciously choose the way we think. Our thoughts are electromagnetic impulses generated in the brain, which have the power of attraction or repulsion. Thought itself is a magnetism, and the realm of thought is magnetic. So high-frequency, loving thoughts will draw high-frequency, loving thought-forms to us. It is our attitude that attracts and moulds the thought-forms around us, and they cluster together on their own plane, their own dimension, their own reality, which is perhaps why, in the realms of science and medicine, we can't really measure thoughts and have a long way to go in trying to do so.

If you observe your thinking and see how it is working, you may notice how certain thought patterns draw other thought patterns to you, how they cluster around you and can close you down. For example, if you have a really strong set of opinions, they will draw their thought-forms around you like a cloak, creating a shield so that your mind will not be open and flexible, and it won't be able to mould and adapt to higher thought-forms, making you stuck.

The mind takes on and works with what is in the heart and the soul. Thoughts that do not contain love can easily become stuck and then stagnate in the chemistry of the body.

Your thoughts need to contain love, because when you expand your thought patterns with loving thoughts, your mind and your aura open up, the clouds move away and you start to feel a clarity and a lucidity, and you feel the heart open and the breath moving into your body and spirit. Your mind is no longer trapped, and it starts to travel into the possibilities of the cosmos. It starts to become truly creative and full of potential to do anything, even merging with the boundless and the infinite.

We need to keep our minds young in that way, not by adding more thoughts, but by sifting. When we read something, or listen to someone's latest theory, or watch an interview or a film, we have to sift all that information. And when we find things that close us down, it is best to let them go, and not attract or draw them in. For instance, if you found yourself among a lot of people arguing in a room, then rather than engaging with those arguments, it is better to watch and listen, and perhaps at some point inject a higher thought, a more open thought to break the chain and the pattern. Then the higher emotions that were blocked by the negative thoughts could be freed.

A clear mind repels doubt and confusion, and once we have cleared our mind and our thoughts, the emotional field begins to open up and we feel relaxed again, experiencing a sense of clarity. Emotions largely rest upon our thinking and rely upon the way we think. That is how, during childhood, when we are very receptive, we are so easily programmed and reprogrammed by the feelings and voices of others, which become our own thoughts and feelings, and our inner voice.

So think about the thought weather that you are creating in your daily life and see how it is programming you, your life and the people around you. See what different kinds of thoughts you can attract by changing the magnetism. You can do this through contemplation. When you contemplate something luminous, something higher, something beautiful, and if you listen and take in thoughts that are of a higher nature, the weather clears and the sun comes out inside you. And when you share that open-mindedness, that open-heartedness and that sunshine, it is infectious to others.

THE SIX STAGES OF TRANSFORMATION – IN SELF, RELATIONSHIPS AND COMMUNITY

The key to experiencing a breakthrough is transformation. I have found that there are six stages to any transformation process within an individual, a relationship, a community or an entire system or organisation.

The first stage is Dissonance. If you take two outputs, and they do not match each other in their energy, this is dissonance. It is common throughout the universe and it happens whenever two or more things are not in harmony, not in synchronisation. In a relationship, if you are aware, you can feel dissonance when it arrives and it is always uncomfortable. Many relationships persist in dissonance with people just reacting to it and never becoming transformed, just going round and round in a loop. It can be the same with communities, governments and countries.

Dissonance is there to tell us something. It is the beginning of a process, and a very magical journey. So it is to be respected, perhaps also even welcomed, in our hearts when we feel it. Dissonance also applies to us as individuals. We can have days when we feel dissonant, when there is something in the stellar field, something in the weather patterns or just something out there that feels dissonant.

Do you remember the physics lesson where you drop two different things into a wave tank, and then you watch the waves coming together and see them colliding and creating an interference frequency? Eventually the patterns begin to harmonise, and it is the same with us. So dissonance is really important as the baseline of all transformation, all creative processes, of evolution itself. It all begins with dissonance.

The second stage is Feedback. When you go to a gig or a performance, somebody may be working with the audio and microphones, and suddenly you get a deafening burst of feedback. You get that really loud, grating sound which is the feedback that is coming out of the dissonance. First comes the dissonance, and then the feedback arrives out of it. And the dissonance can be subtle, so unless you have a finely-tuned awareness, for example, through being a deep meditator, it can be that you are not aware of the dissonance until there is feedback. Dissonance is felt deeply within us and if you are busy about your life, you may not even notice it because you are used to it. Perhaps you are having a bad day and are just ploughing on with things. So, unless you pause, the dissonance will probably go unnoticed. Pausing allows you to tune in and recognise when there is something deeply uncomfortable inside that you need to pay attention to.

In any system or relationship, dissonance creates feedback, which might, for example, be anger erupting out of the dissonance. The relationship or the system then alerts itself to the dissonance and this can be positive or negative, it just depends. You can even look at a negative and turn it into a positive. A burst of anger or irritation in a relationship, or someone losing their cool within a community is a valuable piece of feedback, an alert that is saying there is some dissonance at the core. Even if that person or that behaviour is very challenging, take that feedback on board. It is saying, 'Listen here, there is some dissonance. There is a process under way which is probably going to be uncomfortable. But we need to follow it and listen to it.'

Healthy feedback is when you can say, 'I sense dissonance,' and you do not blame it on anyone. In the negative, shadow state the feedback gets transferred as blame, in the process psychologists call 'transference'.

You transfer the blame of the feedback onto the other person instead of realising that it is just dissonance in the field, and isn't about that person necessarily. It is something passing through the relationship, the individual, the body, the community or the organisation. And that does not mean that suddenly that person who is producing the feedback is very important, or that they are necessarily right. They are just an aspect of the dissonance of the whole. It also does not mean that there is anything 'wrong' with them. It is likely they just have their own personal wounding and they need to be responsible for that. One needs to be responsible for one's feedback. You can give positive feedback and say, *'This isn't working, I didn't like this... I felt like this...'* You own the feedback inside yourself but you offer it with respect and courtesy, and with no blame. That is healthy feedback.

Stage three, Assimilation, is a special one and is kind of magical. Assimilation is when the alchemy starts to occur. The feedback phase is when you become aware of the pattern, and the assimilation phase is when the pattern starts to transmute inside you because you are aware of it. It is uncomfortable because now you are aware that there is a process going on that you are not in control of and you don't know where it is going, and you just have to surrender to it. All transformation at some point reaches this magical phase. And receiving healthy feedback means that you will move through the assimilation process more easily.

When you are in the assimilation phase you can feel the darkness, but you can also see a glimpse of light. In a sense, you are in purgatory. Something is changing inside you, or inside the group, but it has not yet become clear. But you can feel a stirring and it is really important to honour this. It is a chaos zone.

People who are grounded are very good in chaos zones because they can sit within the conflict, look at it, accept it and embrace it. Conflict can be very beneficial, and it can be very creative if it is approached in that way.

Assimilation is a really important phase. The body has to assimilate the information of the transformation, and this can go on for some time. In a relationship, the body of each person and the body of the relationship and its chemistry will make the transformation. If each individual in a relationship is able to maintain courtesy, the transformation may well occur in a very healthy way and much more swiftly. Whereas, if they are fighting and stuck in a feedback loop, the assimilation does not really occur, at least not in a healthy way. Assimilation is different from feedback, because feedback is just the first awareness of dissonance, while assimilation is a complex, internal process.

The fourth phase is called Sharing, which comes out of assimilation like a beam of light. Sharing is about authenticity and sharing authentically how you feel, and you have to go through some assimilation in order to share clearly.

On an individual level, sharing is really about you seeing for the first time what is happening in your life and being able to share it with another person who you trust or love. So speak it, share it, draw it or dance it. Find some way to externalise it so that you can bring it out of yourself and share it. Something needs to emerge from the very internal process of assimilation.

In a relationship the sharing is a critical phase because you have to share without apportioning blame, *'This makes me feel...'* or *'I feel...'* Often in the sharing phase a lot of emotion comes out but it is not in the reactive, feedback stage any more, as it has been processed already.

After some time has passed, the partners in the relationship have had some time to reflect. Perhaps they have been apart and come back together, and then, without being co-dependent, they find they can share in an authentic way.

When sharing in a group or community, it is essential that the sharing is listened to. It is as simple as that. There do not have to be answers. There just has to be the sharing, so that the voices, the complaints, criticisms, hurt, anger, love, all of it, can come out. Everyone has a different view, so all the sharing is of great value, and it needs to come out and be heard.

The fifth stage is called Crystallisation, or Distillation. It is when out of the sharing, suddenly you come to the moment, the realisation within. *'I have gone through this process. I have assimilated, I have shared and I have nothing left I need to put out there.'* You realise that you have learned what you needed to learn, and you are done. Everyone is done and it is almost the end. You have gone through the stages, you have shared and externalised it, and suddenly you understand, *'Aha, now I know what this experience has really been for! I've unlocked the purpose in this suffering, the higher purpose.'* It is wonderful.

In a relationship both partners can look at each other and own their own part of it. They see what they contributed, the good and the bad. The lesson is learned individually, and together they can distill the truth of what has just occurred. Then the relationship becomes a stronger because it has gone through that transformation, and a bonding occurs through that distillation. The sharing is all words, with a lot of emotion and soul stuff coming out, but the distillation is really clear and economical. The emotional stage moves into the quintessence stage, and it is very powerful.

In a community or organisation, there is often one person, or possibly two key people who actually distill the truth of what has happened and put it into words or express it in a really clear way. Many people remain silent because the distillation has occurred inside them and they have understood what the lesson is, and they no longer need to share. It is anchored within them and they feel that they have learned through the experience, and the group also learns through the experience. There is a distillation for everyone, and often a leader or voice for the community will express it eloquently on behalf of the whole.

The sixth and final stage of Transformation is Gratitude. This is the afterglow, because having distilled the lesson, you feel a release. You have moved from dissonance to gratitude. Now, you are suddenly grateful for the dissonance and you think, *'Wow, what a journey!'* and feel that it is done. That phase, that *lila*, that drama, whatever it was or how big it was, whatever crisis that you went through, you now understand it and have let go and moved on. You are stronger for it and feel grateful for the whole process and journey of it.

In a relationship it is the same. What often happens is that love blossoms at that point. Appreciation and respect grow between the pair. They look at each other and feel the love come back, having gone through a phase of no-love and confusion, chaos and assimilation. The depth of gratitude for staying the course can be extraordinary. Their hearts start to beat in harmony again, and they can look the other person in the eyes and say, *'I'm so grateful that you did this or said that or that you stayed with me.'* Then the transformation is complete.

In a community, this is beautiful because a mutual appreciation has come about. The sense of gratitude is felt throughout the community because something has been distilled collectively, as well as each individual distilling things on a personal level. There is a rush of gratitude and a kind of uplift, as the community reaches a level of coherence that was not there before.

All systems, individuals and relationships go through these phases, beginning with a little spark of dissonance. Then the feedback comes and is assimilated through that process of alchemy. There needs to be a sharing of authentic voices, then the distillation and, finally, the gratitude. During one of these processes, in which we all are for most of the time, it is really important to realise that there is a beginning, a middle and an end. You do not have to know exactly where you are, although it is usually pretty clear which phase you are in. It can be very encouraging to identify where you are in the process because it helps you commit to the process through to the end. If you give up, then you never get to the gratitude or the distillation and you will miss the gift of the transformation.

Whether you are applying it to a relationship, a wider community or an organisation or just for yourself, I hope you can begin to see the wonder of this universal process that applies to all life forms and systems. The very cosmos operates according to these stages. Our entire lifetime is there in those six stages, but they can also be contained just in a brief experience within a day. You will see it everywhere, the fundamental, universal pattern woven into every strand of the evolutionary impulse.

GROUNDING
HIGHER FREQUENCIES

An epiphany, a breakthrough into higher consciousness, a peak experience, can really shake us to the core of our being in a positive way. Experiencing euphoric feelings and deep insights into what lies behind the veil of reality opens us to the other realms, to the other dimensions, to the truth. Over time, we realise that the world which we inhabit, that people take as real, is actually just a shadow of what truly is real.

I find higher consciousness to be very compassionate. It gives us a peak experience and then it leaves us alone to work out how to integrate it into our life. However a peak experience comes to us, whether in a retreat, through meditation or yoga, or through working with a plant medicine, the real challenge is how we merge those experiences into our everyday lives.

How we bridge the inner and outer, the mystical realms and ordinary realms, is one of the great questions of our current age. Some teachers don't focus on this, perhaps when the teaching is taking place at an ashram-style retreat when you go there and spend time with the teacher, who is in that world all the time, and then you return to your ordinary life. But we need assimilation time afterwards to absorb our experiences into our day-to-day life. The question is: how do we do it? Since I have to deal with this myself when I leave retreats, I have contemplated it quite a lot.

From a heightened state of consciousness during the retreat, you then return to family and everyday life. That capacity for higher functioning may still be with you when you return, and you have to work out how to handle it. You have to find a way to seamlessly weave that inner shift into a completely different reality, where there are material and emotional commitments and basic responsibilities that have to be dealt with.

Some people try to apply a new discipline to try to retain that state for as long as possible. Perhaps they try some kind of diet, fast or lifestyle change that helps to maintain the clarity, the perception and the thread. These can be positive changes, and in some cases can work. However, what we really need to do is to find ways to normalise the frequency, not just keep it in that pure realm, which it cannot leave. In some respects, this is the opposite to what some teachers might say.

I have an approach that came to me one day as a revelation, and it might be a bit radical –integration through play. Be playful. Don't be too serious or too severe on yourself or on others, and don't expect much of anyone else. Integration through play is about finding ways of bringing higher consciousness into ordinary life. That means you yourself have to be an ordinary person, or play at being an ordinary person.

Personally, I would not be too rigid or strict. I would be the opposite. I would be soft, I would flow, I would be fluid and I would not be too spiritual. I would go out for a drink, maybe eat some pizza, and obviously not go over the top, because, coming from a pure space, you need to start softly. This starts to normalise that higher state into our everyday waking consciousness. I find this approach very helpful, because when we come out of a peak experience and return to everyday reality, we often try to reinforce patterns in our life that keep it alive, and keep it going.

Sometimes we can be tempted to over-share our experiences with those who aren't as receptive, or who cannot possibly understand where we have just been. But peak experiences are not easily put into words, because they need time to be assimilated. So we need to allow ourselves that time for our body, our emotions and our waking reality to assimilate that spiritual experience, and for the higher frequencies that course through our chemistry and our nervous system to be assimilated too.

On the other hand, you might prefer not to talk about your peak experience, even to those close to you. It is up to you. It is for each of us individually to feel into and work out for ourselves. Give yourself that space, yield to the experience and relax, so that those higher frequencies from the heavenly realms can start to come to earth. Try to find playful ways to bring that higher energy into your everyday life – you can't really make a mistake with it. There are no mistakes.

While my children were growing up, I found that I needed to keep up my sense of play, and when I shared things with them it was often very amusing, because I was sharing things from a different reality, and so there was much laughter. It is really healthy to be able to balance the seriousness of what you have experienced with everyday humanity. Playfulness is the start of it. You need that playful spirit, that light-heartedness, and then you can experiment with how to bring the two extremes together into that paradoxical place of wonder.

Integrating through play brings you to a more flowing and harmonious state as you ground those higher frequencies into your everyday life. For those of us who are exploring these realms, it is something to play with.

Some of the highest work that can be done is to bring the path of the spiritual seeker and the path of the everyday together. It is the mark of the spiritual journey of our day to do that. It is a cutting-edge teaching and something I will explore more and more as I move on in my journey as a teacher. It is a great approach to bring into everyday situations, such as your relationships, your working life, or any conflict.

It may be that sometimes you want to return to the spiritual realm, but the trick is to bring the spiritual realm into the mundane, the material life and the emotional life, to breathe it in and bring it alive there. That is the work. Sometimes when I lead meditations, I ask people to open their eyes in the middle of the meditation. We could be in a deep visualisation journey into the body, and then we open our eyes. When you are deep in a realm and suddenly you open your eyes, you stay in that realm, but you are both in and out of it. The more you experience that, the more you create a transition, a seamless bridge between the realms.

Opening your eyes while meditating can be a powerful thing, and when you are not meditating it can help you to drop into the pause, and realise that you are actually in the meditational field even though you might be outside it. You are looking out from the outer world rather than the inner world.

The more you make those bridges, the less the mind distinguishes between inner and outer, and you realise that all the realms can be seamlessly interconnected and bridged.

YOUR BEAUTIFUL MIND

The human mind is amazing. On one hand, it has the capacity to give us ultimate freedom, and on the other it can trap us in so many ways and become a living nightmare.

Awareness of how the mind operates and can be programmed and deprogrammed can open up new realms. One of the ways that the mind can be programmed is through our use of language. Pronouns, those words of identification that we learn from early childhood and take for granted, are interesting. 'I, You, He/She/It, We, You and They' represent six modes of identification, six layers of the mind, and when we consider them, they are extraordinary.

The first layer, 'I', is what I call the Wisdom Mind. We learn and identify with the concept of self from a very young age. The wisdom mind is the capacity of the mind to merge with all creation. It is infinite and eternal, and it interpenetrates all things and all beings. There is nothing that can prevent your mind from going anywhere, and being anything. It is permeated with the wisdom of the universe, and is an icon of the universe. It can access all areas, and therefore can resolve all issues, problems and challenges that we face. This is why I call it the wisdom mind, because when we really understand it, and really see the vast nature of the mind, what it can achieve and what it can know are awesome.

On the other hand, if we look at 'I' in a low-frequency, negative light, it becomes self-sabotaging and self-destructive, and this is the first pattern that can undermine us. 'I' takes on the burden of the whole world, *'I am to blame. I did it. It's me. I am the problem.'* It is a deep sinking into your own misery because you take it all on yourself. You take the full weight of the world onto your shoulders, and out of that can come difficulties with self-esteem, self-love and self-worth, which can lead to self-sabotaging behaviours, and even self-harm, potentially. But remember that this is the wisdom mind, so at its highest level 'I' also has the capacity to know *I am love*, which is the highest capacity that any human being has. 'I am love' is the great statement of the universe – of the wisdom mind.

The Christ principle is *I am love*, and the one who can live *I am love* is a truly wise, limitless being. The wisdom mind has the capacity to break out and move through the patterns of self-sabotage that are imprinted in us. This is the journey of the 'I', the first mind.

The second layer is 'You', in the singular form. This I call the Freedom Mind. The freedom mind is awesome as well. It finds freedom in relationships, through loving another on a one-to-one basis, through connection, intimacy, and looking into another person's eyes, really seeing them and realising that there is more than 'I', because 'I' encompasses more than just what is inside yourself. 'I' is also what is inside the other, inside the 'you'.

The indigenous people of Australia have additional pronouns, on top of the six, and the one that I love is 'we two' or 'us two', which are a bit like 'you' because they have a feeling of intimacy, but they are also different. 'You' is bridging the gap between us. The freedom comes through loving, intimacy, and the connection between all beings. One individual unit connects to another, and realises that, *It wasn't all about me. I'm not to blame. There is more to this.*

At the lower frequencies, the 'you' falls prey to accusation. So whereas the 'I' can self-sabotage, look inward and curl up inside itself, the 'you' projects the blame outward. *'You're to blame! You!'* The 'you' accuses directly, and all the passion of 'you' can then pour out into a relationship and can become angry and destructive. *'You did it! You!'* And it requires the other person to be on the end of the phone or an email, or right in front of you.

It is very common to see blame projected onto the other as relationships break up. We project the blame from ourselves so that we don't have to feel it, because we are afraid of the self-sabotage. So we blame the other, and this creates all kinds of conflicts in the world, and relationships that don't end well.

The greatest beauty of the freedom mind is in its highest statement, 'I love you.' In every language there is a word or an expression for 'I love you', and it is probably the most beautiful statement you can utter to another person (is there anything greater?). It is selfless, and where freedom lies. The freedom mind connects through that intimacy and transparency, in giving another person your full heart and your trust. So, *'You did it'* becomes *'I love you. I forgive you'*. And really you are forgiving yourself, but you are externalising that as love. *'I forgive you.'* It is beautiful. There is a whole story contained in the freedom mind of 'you'.

The third layer, 'He, She and It', I call the Joyous Mind. 'He, she and it' are interesting because they require a relationship to talk about them, or for a writer to describe. 'He did this, he did that. He went on to win a gold medal.' It is the storytelling aspect of the joyous mind, which is able to see others in a more objective way and then to journey through and explore all of creation: the animals, the birds, the bees, the trees, the hills, the rivers, the ocean, the sun and the stars. 'It' looks at the world, takes it all in and is saturated with the beauty all around.

The joyous mind can also become the complaining mind, where the blame is transferred to a third party. *'He is to blame!' 'She did it!'* Again, the blame is projected out, but it is not projected directly into the eyes of another person in an argument, as an accusation. It is projected as a complaint or as gossip, *'Have you heard what he did?!'*

When we complain, we strip the world of its joy, because it is another victim pattern. We blame and project outside ourselves, and even though these are very human patterns and part of our humanity, each one is a journey that we somehow have to go on. And we then come back to the joyous mind, thinking instead, *'I forgive him, I forgive her.'* It then becomes *'He is love, she is love,'* which is a big realisation, and very different from *'I love you.'*

When you say, *'I love her, I love him, I love it,'* you are seeing from a distance that the person or that thing is not what your negative mind believed them to be. That little bit of distance is magic, because you are not directly engaging with them. You realise that everyone is like you and has the same difficulties as you. Joy comes from realising that you are not alone. *'He had the same experience as I did. I really am not alone. It helped me understand, it helped me forgive,'* whatever 'it' might be.

The fourth layer, 'We' I call the Compassionate Mind. This is realising that we are 'we', and that everything we look at: the 'he, she and it', the 'you' looking in the eyes, and the 'I' on its own, are all part of a greater 'we'. That realisation is a huge shift in consciousness, and you see that the pronouns are like octaves that resonate with each other. 'I' and 'we' resonate, 'you' singular and 'you' plural resonate, and 'he, she, it' and 'they' resonate. So 'I' becomes 'we', and wisdom becomes compassion.

The compassionate mind is able to understand through empathy, because 'we' isn't just looking at someone from a distance. It is an understanding that the other person is me, they are inside me, and I am them. That leads to compassion, which leads to resonance, which leads to empathy. 'He, she and it', however, understand through sympathy, because you are looking at that person with understanding, *'Ah, that person had the same journey, the same pain, the same struggle as me, and I can relate to that. This makes me feel happier, because I'm not the only one.'*

In the negative aspect 'we' becomes misery, hopelessness and futility, *'We are all to blame... We did this... We're destroying the planet...'* Of course, conversely, it could also say, *'we can save it,'* but the negative side always collapses into the 'we'. There are those times when we want to drag other people into our hopelessness, into our 'we', and as the saying goes, 'misery loves company'. This can lead to a different kind of collapse, where there is even less hope, because everyone is involved and identifying with it. Then we don't hear any more messages of hope, so we don't resonate with them. *'Even 'we' can't save the world.'* We blame it on ourselves as a whole, and that is really heavy.

The beginning of the journey towards compassion is realising that we are a 'we', and we have the capacity to awaken as a collective, not just as individuals. So, yes, we are to blame to a degree, but also we have the capacity to rise up and transmute what we have done, to fix the problems we have caused, everyone working together to bring beauty back into the world, working as a collective: as societies, families and relationships. Then it becomes *'We are love'*, which is possibly the greatest statement that any human can utter. Because while I said that *'I am love'* is the great statement of the universe, there is nothing more intimate than 'We are love' as everyone is part of the whole 'we'. 'We are all love' is the compassionate mind.

Then we have the plural form of 'You', which is an odd one. I call it the Abundant Mind, because it is a way of looking out through the eyes and directly connecting with the multiple beings and creatures out there, but in an intimate way, 'You, all of you out there.' There is always a distance here, but there is also an interpenetration.

'You' plural is the abundant nature of creation. We look out and we can see there is you, and there is you, and also you and you and you and... There are so many! There is a wonderful abundance, a proliferation of connection, of relationship, an interconnected community of being. 'You' plural sees how everything is interconnected, and the abundance and prosperity that creation can produce. You can look up into the cosmos and see all those countless stars, all those other yous, and know they are all part of it, too.

On the negative side, 'you' plural can become delusional and twisted, 'You are all to blame. You did it, all of you! I'm going to take my revenge on you.' It becomes a complex inside us, a vendetta, even, where you play out a pattern in your life where there is a paranoia underneath which makes you think that everyone is looking at you, 'You're all looking at me. I've got to behave in a certain way. I've got an expectation of myself, a pressure, because all of you are seeing me.' There is a huge pressure to be something that you are not, and to narrow down the abundance.

You get caught in deluded ideas of what you think you should look like and how you should behave, and all the other 'shoulds'. And it can be tyrannical, because 'you' plural is about leadership. It is the view of leaders, and it can also take advantage of you, 'You, all of you! You should follow me!

Follow me and I will help you. I can lead you.' 'You' plural talks to everyone like that.

The other aspect of it is, *'You are all love,'* which is like the Messiah talking. *'You are all love'* might sound arrogant, but leadership can be like that. It is not that you have to say, *'You are all love,'* but it is a healthy projection. *'Every one of you, every little atom; you are all love,'* this is the abundance of the cosmos, and out of 'you' plural come the great leaders and voices of humanity. In the same way, a really great musician or writer is connecting individually with all the different singular 'yous', and the words they speak and the music they make are going to touch all the different 'yous', because they reach into your heart. There is a real beauty in the abundant mind.

Finally, we come to 'They', the Silent Mind, because 'they' has true objectivity. 'They' looks at everything, all things, all beings, and sees it all on a screen of consciousness. It looks at the thoughts passing across, *'Look at that thought. There goes a thought. There goes another one, and another. Look at them all passing in front of us.'* Everything is just a screen and the projection on it, and there is a distance, a silence where nothing needs to complicate life, and everything becomes simple again. In a way, this is a return to the joyous mind, because in that silence, in that witnessing, an awe-inspiring joy wells up. It might also be called the awestruck mind. We are all figments of mind, and all those thoughts that are passing before the screen of this consciousness, are all 'theys'. So there is an extraordinary witnessing in the silent mind.

In the negative frequency 'They' becomes conspiracy, *'They are all to blame. They did it. It's them, the men in black, the government, the aliens, the cabal conspiring to get me, the gods.'* Whatever it is, there are a lot of 'them', and it is a negative projection that 'they' have power and are trying to usurp us.

'They' thinks, *I've seen them. I understand them. I've seen through them. They are out to get us.* Of course, there are some elements of truth in these thoughts, as is often the way with conspiracy. But if you make conspiracy your world view, your mind will never be silent. It will never trust, never sit back and just watch the projections as another part of history taking place, and let it all just pass by.

If you are caught up with conspiracies, you have projected your identity into the game. Then you may feel as if you have the power to do something about it, and you are off on a mission, *'Let's go get them!'* You can see this in the world today, in all the 'thems' looking at the other 'thems', whether it is two opposing political parties facing each other, or women and men looking at each other, saying, *'It's them! It's them!'*

Whichever side you are on, when you look together as one group and look at another group, schisms and fractures are created. So look deep into these patterns. They are woven into the infrastructure of our brain, of our neurology, and you can be caught in them. If you see through the patterns, you will understand that, ultimately, what 'they' sees is *'they are all love'.* Every thought is love, every being is love, every atom is love. It is all witnessed as love from a place of silence.

A silent mind is the only thing that can see through the delusions, the hopelessness, the complaining, the accusations, the self-sabotage and the conspiracy. And then all the six layers, the six minds, which are really one, come together in perfect resonance.

The silent mind realises that it is the wisdom mind because it is infinite, and then the wisdom mind realises it is the freedom mind, *'I love you. I am love.'* Then the joyous mind wells up, *'He is love, she is love, it is love,'* and then 'we', the compassionate mind, *'We can do anything because we are love.'*

Then 'you', the abundant mind, *'All of you are love,'* has a level of intimacy that connects. Finally, the silent mind, *'They are love.'* 'They' comes back to 'I' and the circle is complete. All these different minds are really just one mind. But our language patterns have taught us to divide ourselves into these illusory fragments, when in fact there is just one whole.

Perhaps now you can see through some of the patterns that you may be experiencing and may even be caught in. Seeing through these veils can really help you to find the vast and wider minds: the wisdom mind, the freedom mind, the joyous mind, the compassionate mind, the abundant mind and the silent mind. It can also help to understand and increase your capacity for forgiveness, for love and for joy.

We are here to play roles in the theatre of life, and many of those roles have integrity, and their own dharma and karma. Whichever role you find yourself in, play it to the hilt, but see through it at the same time. Because there are injustices in the world, and a part of the human journey is to take on those injustices as we see them. That is a valuable and wonderfully empowering thing to do.

Each one of these minds is a journey – a journey to freedom – to break through into a wider sphere of consciousness. So every step is of value. You have to make the journey to achieve the freedom. It is important to play the role that you are playing and to see what you are seeing. But at the same time be able to see through the veil that you may be caught in, because then you can play your role, without being overly attached to the theatre itself.

In other words, you know you are wearing a costume and that gives you the freedom to play your role well without being caught in the drama itself, because then you are free.

Each of us should feel free to play the role that we wish to play and at the same time realise that all roles are ultimately illusions – costumes that we discard when we die and return into the wisdom mind, the silent mind. So embrace your role and enjoy it.

SADNESS, ALONENESS AND CREATIVITY

There are times when we are with someone, and times when we are alone. You may find yourself longing for more solitude and space when you are with someone, and you may find yourself at times longing for intimacy when you are alone. Often the nature of humanity is to long for the other side. Your Spiritual Quotient, your SQ, which is really your heart and your soul, speaks of this very human dilemma.

Having a healthy SQ means entering into a profound relationship with your aloneness. The beauty and the ache of aloneness in life are played out through the seasons of our relationships. The following passage is taken from 'The Gene Keys Golden Path – Love – The Venus Sequence'.

Aloneness and Loneliness:

'Aloneness brings its own gifts, and one of these is an honouring of the sadness of life, as well as its joy. As you learn to contemplate life in more and more depth, you will come into touch with the inner fugue played by joy and sadness. There are times in life when we are called to enter into phases of deep melancholy. Sometimes there are reasons and sometimes there are not. At such times we often ache with a kind of cosmic loneliness whose roots seem to go so far down into our depths, that we wonder if we can ever be truly happy again.

Such times can be difficult if we don't manage to maintain a sense of wonder and creativity in our lives. Without the creative process, there is a danger that we are pulled into the black hole of melancholy, which then sucks the life force away from us and leaves us feeling depressed. Once depression sets in, it can be very challenging to build up enough inner velocity to re-emerge.

Almost all of life's greatest works of art, music, literature and drama have emerged out of the genius of melancholy, or out of human beings who have allowed melancholy a deep place in their inner lives. If we are to rise to the peaks of consciousness, we must also hold a place for the nadir inside us. This is a beautiful and vulnerable process. Your SQ is a delicate balance of your Intelligence Quotient, your IQ, and your Emotional Quotient, your EQ, your passion and your reason, of shadow and light, of intimacy and aloneness, of loss and love.

When you feel the call of your aloneness, then you must find a way to honour it, and creativity is the most vital and transformative way when you are following the Path of Love. Through creativity you maintain a state of communion with your fellow man. Others can see into your being and take solace from the fact that there is something emerging there'.

It is a beautiful notion that an absolutely essential part of every human journey is to embrace our aloneness, our loneliness, and to go right into that inner solitude. As the poet Rilke said, *'To walk inside yourself and meet no one for hours – that is what you must be able to attain.'* To experience days in silence, in the vacant space inside us that many of us fear, and yet our creativity springs from that inner space. We just have to have the courage to embrace it and let it become a part of us. If we let it swallow us in its fathomlessness, then the path of depression will be a difficult one.

So, when we find ourselves in that empty space, we have to learn to embrace it and use its energy. If you wake up in the morning and you feel that emptiness, instead of immediately trying to run from it, you could spend some time contemplating it. Go into it, find the softness around it, see that there is something beautiful inside it that may emerge during your day. There is an ember in there, an ember of light, of beauty. We need to find that ember and follow it, and then release it.

There is usually a reason for feeling sad, but it is also OK to be sad for no reason. Feeling sad is part of who we are. The lows are part of the experience of being human just as much as the highs. It is all about inner awareness, the equanimity that we must have so that we can hold the extremes and all the places in between. When we have equanimity, it settles us, so that we do not swing from one end to the other, back and forth, and we are not attached to being at the high end. We can just allow life to play its music through us, and experience the mystery of that. We do not get to control it, because it is the fugue and the melody of life.

THE FEAR TRACKER

We each carry a finite store of fear inside our bodies which is related to our karma. As we go through life and evolve, we work through our karma, and that store of fear inside us can be transmuted. The fear creates the illusion that we are separate beings. It creates a duality where we seem to be a 'you' and an 'I' – where we appear to be separate. But when we remove that separation, there is no 'you' or 'I', just love, light and interconnection.

The fear is crying out to us to transform it, so we have to keep track of it and be with it when it appears. We can do this in two ways. One way is to wait for fear to appear, and since it is everywhere, you will soon find it, as life provides it over and over again by holding up a mirror. Of course, love is mirrored too, but because fear is in the body, it underlies everything. The other way is, instead of waiting for the fear to manifest, we go hunting for it and we learn to actually track it down. We become a fear tracker. We ask, *'Where does fear live in my life? Where am I most afraid? Where am I most unhappy? Where is there most pain?'* Then we go towards that pain and fear.

We hunt that fear down with our love, gentleness, acceptance and contemplation. We find the fear in our body, and we open to it and acknowledge it and learn from it. We make a space for the fear to be felt, to be listened to and heard, although we don't have to understand it.

Fear is often multi-levelled, some of it coming from this life, rooted in childhood trauma, and some coming from our ancestors' trauma, loss or grief. Some fear is from far, far back in our racial genetic memory and we carry it on behalf of humanity as a collective fear. This is the deepest fear – the collective wound of all beings, going right back to the beginning of time. Using this method, we hunt the fear, and when we find it, we give it space.

It is important to realise that all fear is finite, and this is an important thing to celebrate, because when you know that, you know there is an end to it. You must always keep that end in sight in your heart, even when you are deep in the midst of it. You allow it in, and you offer it up for the betterment of humanity, or whatever your heart wishes to offer, and then you transmute it day after day.

We have to keep going specifically to those places where fear appears to be strongest, and we just watch it. That is all you have to do. It is like standing on the edge of a cliff. You don't jump off the cliff. You just stand there. You just go to the edge and look at your fear. That is all this practice requires. Just looking at the fear and being with it will transform it, gradually, over the years.

Through this practice, we are transforming finite reservoirs of fear, and one day, we will get to the last few atoms of fear left inside us. These are the most stubborn ones. We must give these remnants our ultimate gentleness as they disappear into the vast light of the consciousness that lives inside us, behind the fear.

So, I invite you to become a hunter and go and find your fear. Don't wait for it to find you. And when you have found your fear, be gentle with it as it transmutes, and you will soon find a miracle unravelling before your very heart.

ANTIDOTE FOR ANXIETY

Anxiety is a very common disorder which is suffered by many people. For some, it is experienced just occasionally during crisis or difficulty. For others, it is a permanent affliction and can be debilitating and extremely difficult. Those who experience it can get into loop-thinking, which enhances the unsafe feelings and further stokes all the horrors that come with deeper levels of anxiety.

It is tempting to think of anxiety as a mental condition that can be handled by thinking about things differently. But my understanding of anxiety is that it is in the cells of the body, and is primarily physical, although obviously it also has an emotional and mental component. Ultimately this suggests that anxiety is best addressed through the physical body, since it is a frequency and a vibration that the physical body is afflicted by, whose secondary affects are in our emotions and our mind.

I have a very simple suggestion for dealing with anxiety, in the form of an exercise where you place your palms on your belly and just breathe. This is where the anxiety stems from, as well as where all illness and disease ultimately stem from at an energetic level. So if you want to address a problem, the ideal is to go to the core, to the belly.

Here is what you do: you place your hands on your stomach and begin to breathe gently and lightly. Bring your awareness into your palms and allow the breath to then drop down steadily deeper into your belly. This happens without your trying. If you feel really anxious, you could also softly circle your palms, letting them move round in small circles at first, and then gradually making them bigger. Preferably move in a clockwise direction, since that is how peristalsis and digestion flow around the belly. But you can move them in any direction, so go with what feels right.

This simple technique will begin to relax the whole system. It communicates to the cells of the body the feeling that it everything is OK. We have to do this through our intent, and even though it may feel far from OK, the idea is to communicate reassurance to our body. You reassure your body as you would a distressed child, as though telling it, *'It's all right. It's going to be all right, it's going to be fine.'*

You are not communicating with any sense of identity, or with a past affliction, or any idea that you have in your mind about why you think you feel anxious, or any worry about the future, or anything like that. You are just conveying pure reassurance to the core of your body. You are letting the soft animal of your body know that it is OK, that it is safe here, even when it feels the opposite. The body at its core essentially knows this truth already, so you are just reminding it, and the more you do this simple exercise, the more you will see that your body begins to remember. And as your body begins to remember, your breathing starts to move a bit deeper down.

It is really important not to force your breathing in any way. There must be no forcing in this at all. This is just a pure and gentle listening exercise, where you are touching your own belly, and allowing your breath to move with your palms, whether you move your palms, or hold them still, or both. And as you allow them to move, or you allow them to be still, just gently allow the breath to start naturally moving down to where your palms are.

You will find over time, as you begin to feel better, that you also begin to feel softer. You begin to tune into a deeper rhythm and, as this happens, your emotions start to settle, and your mind falls quieter.

You can use this technique as often as you want, and for as long as you want. If you are suffering from anxiety, I recommend that you do it often. You could do it every time you think of it. Soon you will begin to tune into a space behind the anxiety, a feeling of, *'It's all right, I'm safe, it's safe to be in this body.'* As you feel that more and more deeply you will come into a cellular memory of trust, the trust that your body has in life, and in the timing and the rhythm of life. It is that deep, core cellular trust that you are approaching when you do this very simple exercise.

Whenever you feel upset, nervous, anxious, or any of those kinds of difficult perturbing feelings, try this simple exercise and allow your breathing to return to a more natural, rhythmic state. Depending on how deep the anxiety is, take your time accordingly. It is a gradual process, so you don't have to be in a hurry. You could do this for weeks, months, even years, and it will slowly, bit by bit, start to chip away at whatever pattern is causing the anxiety. You are just rubbing the sacred lamp of your belly and allowing the light to shine there again, and it will begin to shine in the core of every cell.

Ultimately, you will begin to feel calm and relaxed, and your belly will soften and open. You don't need to understand it. Just know that it can take you all the way through to healing that anxiety.

All that is required is patience, gentleness, listening and surrender. The more you do it, the more relaxed and blissful you will eventually begin to feel, until you reach a point where you can just place your hands on your belly and feel it instantly.

If you experience anxiety, this exercise could really help you. I hope you enjoy doing it and the simplicity of it.

My love goes towards you, wherever you are and whatever levels of anxiety you are feeling.

DEALING WITH TEENAGERS

This is called 'Dealing with Teenagers', but it is not for parents alone. This is for everyone, including parents, because it is about dealing with the teenager inside each of us, and seeing how our minds can contract around uncomfortable emotions. It is interesting that in order to unlock the deeper currents of our emotions, we must first unlock our minds. This is explored in the Shadow of the IQ Gene Key in your Venus Sequence, which is an integral part of the Gene Keys Golden Path programme.

The common story is that at some point we began to believe ourselves unworthy of love. Out of this deep-seated belief we developed a narrow way of thinking and behaving that often emerges when we feel emotionally threatened or uncomfortable. For some though, the pattern just emerges when it emerges, and you might just wake up one day and there it is. But, however it is triggered, this pattern develops in each of us through the primary imprinting cycle of the Mental Body from age 14 to 21, during our seven-year teenage cycle.

When you contemplate the Shadow of your IQ through working with your Gene Keys, you become aware of the ways of thinking that can lock you down and hold your emotions back from emerging or coming out fluidly. You can observe that part of your mind that causes your emotions to not be expressed in a healthy way, and instead come out in unhealthy expressions such as blame, arrogance, accusation, self-pity, shame, guilt or manipulation; or it could be that this part of your mind simply cuts itself off. These are all just neural pathways, though, and you can therefore re-program them.

On the other side of the Shadow is the Gift of the IQ, and its gifts are manifold. Once the mind has been freed from holding back our fuller maturity, an enormous amount of energy is released through our body and brain. So we have to be continually alert for and aware of the shadow pattern whenever we experience emotional discomfort. The good news is that as you open your mind once again to the possibility that you are worthy of love, then you become more intelligent! This relates to your IQ, which represents your mental alacrity, but it also involves optimism, which is not part of the average IQ test.

Optimism is not the same as positive thinking. It comes from drawing in high-frequency thought-forms, and it is the nature of a truly open mind. So the Gift of your IQ is more than just about being clever and intellectual, it is about open-circuit thinking. **The mark of true intelligence is the certainty that you are fully worthy of love.** During the Venus Sequence you learn about your true IQ, and about the subtlety of the Mental Body and the importance of the qualities we draw into it, and how, in opening up to the cosmic mind, those higher thought-forms open up our thinking.

The Venus Sequence can reconnect us to that expansive teenage mind we once had, that was open to all possibilities, concepts and ideas, no matter how 'out there' they might be. That mind is on the edge of the wisdom mind, and so we have to reclaim that openness of thinking and rekindle it.

The way to deal with teenagers or the teenager inside yourself is through keeping a really open mind. When you feel that you are worrying, 'There is something wrong here, I am going to fix this,' try to soften those judgement patterns. The open mind does not worry. The open mind looks for the possibility, rather than the shadow. From there, the emotions start to move again, the love starts to move, and out of that a solution is always found. Do you see the difference? If you approach with a tense mind, the solution will never be the right solution. Whereas if you open to expanding and willing to drop those judgements, then you soften, the heart begins to move and perhaps tears start to come. Then you can approach any teenager, or the teenager inside you in the right way.

We are multi-aged, and the teenagers inside us need to be treated with respect, openness and understanding, just as much as the teenagers in our outer life. If you can understand and relate to your teenager like that, your inner teenager or your outer teenager, they will feel that openness around you. Then they will be able to express whatever it is they express, or also not express it, because that is also their freedom.

The point is that you won't feel pressure inside you to do or fix something. You can show understanding and just be available for them. Then the love will begin to flow, and in time the love will begin to find solutions. Love always finds the solutions. Love always finds the way.

JORGE LUIS BORGES

I have many favourite writers who have influenced me, and one that I used to read a lot when I was younger was Jorge Luis Borges, an Argentinian who lived from 1899 to 1986. He was a giant of both Argentine and world literature, an absolutely wonderful writer and I have a little story about him here.

A young writer once asked Borges if he could meet him. The great man was by then blind and nearing the end of his life, but he agreed to the meeting. The young man said that reading Borges' works had given him a happiness and beauty that he couldn't find in life. The young writer, whose name was German Kral, went on to become a filmmaker and made a documentary, 'Images of the Absence' in which he talked about his memories of his meeting with Borges. Apparently Borges had given him some very moving advice:

'The task of art is to transform what is continually happening to us. To transform all these things into symbols, into music, into something that can last in man's memory. That is our duty. If we don't fulfil it, we feel unhappy. A writer or any artist has the sometimes joyful duty to transform all of that into symbols. These symbols could be colours, forms or sounds.

For a poet, the symbols are sounds, and also words, fables, stories, poetry. The work of a poet never ends. It has nothing to do with working hours. You are continually receiving things from the external world. These must be transformed, and eventually will be transformed. The revelation can appear at any time. A poet never rests, he's always working, even when he dreams.

Besides, the life of a writer is a lonely one. You think you're alone, and as the years go by, if the stars are on your side, you may discover that you're at the centre of a vast circle of invisible friends whom you will never get to know, but who love you, and that is an immense reward.'

I love that last line. Sometimes, I feel that is me, in the centre of a circle of invisible friends whom I will never get to know but who, I feel, send me their love. Obviously, what Borges is talking about is high art. But we are all artists in different ways. Our job is to transform the things that happen to us into potent symbols, in whatever way we can, inside us.

When something becomes a symbol then it also can become a teaching. It does not matter what form the symbol takes, because as he says, it could be a colour in a painting or a sound in music. It could become a design for a garden that you are working on, or many things that you bring into the world. You bring the unknown, and you make it visible in some way. So in that sense we are all poets, and our work never ends until we die. At any time, revelations and insights can appear.

I encourage you to look into the work of Borges. There are some wonderful short stories that he wrote in a collection called 'The Book of Sand' or 'El Libro de Arena'. There are some amazing, epic stories in there. They are very short, but rich with potent symbols which he does not explain. He leaves that to us. That is the power of a symbol. If you try to explain it away, it loses its magic and its mystery, because its meaning is different for each person.

So, whenever you are involved in contemplation of anything of a higher nature, let the symbols sink in, and your contemplation will open them up and extract the juices over time.

Thank you, Borges, wherever you are. You must have been a wonderful man.

FRAGMENTS OF LIGHT
CHAPTER 3

THE ART OF CONTEMPLATION

In the fast-paced world of today, you might worry about finding time for something like contemplation. But the beauty of it is that contemplation can happen in little pauses in our day and it goes on all the time in the background, even when we are busy.

These moments of calm and lucidity seem like an oasis in the relentlessness of our busy lives, and we find that we can tap into a universal wisdom that can help us make sense of anything that comes our way. At the deepest level, contemplation becomes part of us and then our whole life can be transformed.

HARVESTING PAUSES
THE ART OF CONTEMPLATION – PART 1

Pausing is the foundation of the art of contemplation. It sounds like the simplest thing in the world, and it is a simple discipline, but it is hard in the beginning. Here is an excerpt from my book 'The Art of Contemplation'.

Harvesting Pauses:

'The technique of pausing involves nothing more than noticing life's natural pauses and then simply enjoying them. Everything in nature pauses. If you watch any bird, animal or insect, you will see it regularly pause for no apparent reason. Actually, there are many reasons for pausing. When you stop in your particular activity, you become more aware of your environment. You also become more aware of your inner environment. You may suddenly realise you are tired, or that your mind was spinning, or that your breathing has become shallow and laboured. Pauses like this often invite a physical sigh, as the body remembers to draw a deep breath, and let go of some tension.

The first stage of the technique of pausing therefore involves finding and spotting the natural pauses that open up before you each day. Once you notice them, you can harvest them like fresh apples picked from the bough. Pauses are here to be enjoyed.

How long is a pause? A pause can be as short as a single breath or it can be much longer. You can begin this technique by finding as many short pauses in your day as you can. For example, when you are sitting looking at your screen, perhaps answering an email or a text, before you rush from one response to the next, try taking a few breaths between each one and perhaps look up and take in the environment around you.

Another example might be when you are in your car and you get to the traffic lights just as they turn red. Instead of feeling frustrated or irritated, you could look at it another way. Life has just gifted you a pause. In that pause you can enter the field of contemplation.

These very simple techniques can have far reaching effects in your life. A day filled with pauses is a calm and measured day. Nothing ever becomes overwhelming or causes you too much stress. What's more, when you get to the end of such a day, even though your body may be tired, your mind will still feel clear and uncluttered, leading to a deep sleep and a fine morning the following day.'

Pausing is a really enjoyable technique and it could not be simpler. The challenge for the modern world is to try to find the pauses in your everyday life. It does not matter if you have a very busy life or a quiet and relaxing one. Find the pauses. When you find them, it is like finding diamonds, because each pause opens up a possibility through silence and a connection to your inner essence. This essence within you is always completely at ease and is simply a witness to the passage of your life. The more we therefore rest in that essence, the more peaceful we are, the more connected we feel, and the greater capacity we have for breakthroughs.

Breakthroughs can be about all kinds of things, and as a result of them, we begin to see things with a clear mind and an open heart, and then patterns can really change in our lives. Sometimes negative patterns can even change on their own, just through filling our day with pauses.

When you fill your day with pauses, you are actually giving yourself more time. It is an amazing paradox that the more you pause, the more time you create for yourself.

You will see that your day runs far more efficiently than when you were racing ahead from the beginning to the end, hardly aware of what was going on around you while you were absorbed in the stream of busyness. So, fill that busyness with the little lights of pauses. Learn how to harvest them, and you will see a miracle growing in your life.

POETIC PAUSES, PAUSING FOR BEAUTY
THE ART OF CONTEMPLATION – PART 2

The art of contemplation begins with pausing, and it is up to us to find these moments where we can take a pause. There are many different ways we can do this, and we may have to be quite creative to carve out these moments in our day. It can sometimes be a bit of a dance. Here is some more insight from 'The Art of Contemplation'.

Creating Pauses:

'A major part of the art of contemplation is to engage your own spirit of creativity. It's up to you how you create more pauses in your day. Pausing is a form of self-discipline and takes some time to re-imprint the habit in your life. However, once we have begun the process it can be both fun and very revealing.

There are many types of pauses. Pausing doesn't necessarily mean that you have to stop moving and remain still. This is only one aspect of pausing. Another type of pause is the transitionary pause between one event in our life and the next. For example, walking to work can be a pause. It all depends on how you walk. If you rush headlong down the street while at the same time as gazing at your phone, this is not creating a pause. If, however, you saunter along the road at a leisurely pace, enjoying the fact that you are truly savouring this moment, then perhaps your lips will curl into a smile and for a few moments you will feel truly free and relaxed.'

Taking a pause during a busy day does not mean that you have to stop your outer activity, but there is a gap in your inner activity. You can carry on doing what you are doing, but suddenly you do it with awareness and mindfulness, and the activity changes subtly.

A pause can also be a break, simply a moment to close your eyes, take a breath and physically stop. To make the opportunities for more pauses, you may have to get quite creative and rethink your day somewhat. If you are heading out somewhere, you could give yourself a bit more time, just so you give yourself the luxury to meander a little.

In our modern world, it can feel a bit naughty, in a way, to organise your life so that you can drift a bit. Yet it is OK to give yourself an extra five minutes to meander, saunter or linger – all lovely English words that invoke the idea of pausing in movement. It is also really important to pause between switching activities. All too often we rush headlong from one activity to another. See if you can instead use the natural break to create a pause between one activity and the next.

The more we find these breaks in the natural patterns of flow in our lives, the more poetic, more leisurely, more romantic and more relaxed our life becomes, and because we notice more around us, we start to fully appreciate the aesthetics, the beauty and the play of light. Even on a grey day, you can find exquisiteness in the tonality of the light as it falls on a branch or on someone's face, or on the dish cloth. You are seeing the sacred in the everyday.

If you have ever worked with plant medicines, you may remember moments where you see absolute beauty in the most mundane things, simply because you are more dialled in. But this is not something that requires any chemical change. It actually can be baked into your life simply through learning the art of contemplation.

Poetic pauses, where we pause in order to imbibe beauty, are something that we can develop inside us. They are an aspect of our perception that we can enhance through the self-discipline that comes from the art of contemplation, which is an art, not a science. It is an amazing process that we have to go back to anew each day.

In contemplation, we have to sculpt our day, our life, according to the poetic laws that we find and see operating around us. Even in the hubbub and the craziness of the city, there is great beauty to be found in the dreariest office or in the exhausted faces on the train going home. We can always see it, if we look deeply enough. We just have to pay attention, and maybe come off our screens for a moment. When we have seen it, we might feel a little bit of awe, and perhaps a little revelation that this is what life is actually for.

The first of all the Gene Keys is Beauty, and that is why, first and foremost, we are here to love beauty, not in the sense of wanting to look beautiful, but to see and perceive beauty everywhere, within everything. Even in ugliness or in pain, there are fragments, little moments of beauty, and the art of contemplation teaches us how to see them. That is what makes it one of the most treasured and overlooked of all the Arts.

So go out there, sculpt a poetic life using the art of contemplation, and you will see that you are spreading light wherever you go.

PIVOTING
THE ART OF CONTEMPLATION – PART 3

The three stages in the art of contemplation: pausing, pivoting and merging, are really one technique because they are contained in and emerge from each other. Pivoting, the second layer in the art of contemplation, comes from pausing. Pivots occur within pauses, and so as you create more inner space within yourself and in your life, you increase the possibility of pivotal moments. These are moments of breakthrough when you see that a pattern which has been running inside you, perhaps for years or even your whole life, has unconsciously been undermining you in some way or creating stress or friction inside your body, and perhaps even other people's lives.

During a breakthrough, you can suddenly see that pattern in a different light, and you see it fully for the first time. This creates the potential for a pivotal experience. That change in view, that paradigm shift, leaves you feeling different and having reached that awareness, it is hard for you to return to that same old pattern.

We carry patterns like these from childhood and, unless we are really deep seekers or contemplators, they can keep on running, and they ruin our lives. They steal our energy like vampires that cling to us, robbing us of our joy and our vitality. Sometimes it can also be that we wake up in the morning and just feel down for no obvious reason. Here is an example taken from 'The Art of Contemplation'.

Pivoting:

'You are feeling emotionally low. You have lost touch with any sense of joy or deeper purpose in life. You feel disconnected from others and you don't know how to get back to a brighter place.

Instead of trying to distract yourself from the discomfort, you create a pause, a space inside yourself so that you can look at your inner state with honesty.

On deeper self-reflection you realise that the state you are in is a deep numbness. You remember that this is not unique to you but universal to all human beings. From this place of self-compassion, you go further into yourself, into your heart, until you find the tiniest flame.

There is always a small flame in the midst of the numbness. You cradle this precious flame, like a tiny spark on a cold winter's night. You gently fan the flame with patience until it grows inside you. This may take time, even several days. But over time, your awareness and courage help to bring this flame back to life. You begin to feel human again. You feel warmth and hope dawn inside you. You have made self-compassion and love the pivot for a total change in awareness, and having done it once, you draw strength from knowing you can do it again whenever you need. You have learned to bring your heart back to life.'

Pivoting is particular to the heart and tends to be an emotional experience. So while an insight is a mental breakthrough, pivoting is an emotional breakthrough where the heart opens and we soften, remembering more of ourselves and unlocking more vitality. Pivoting is a technique that mostly happens on its own, and although it starts with an act of will, as in the above example, you still have to make the decision to stop and inquire deeper. You still need to have the courage to look at the discomfort.

So you close your eyes, you go within and feel it. Whatever it is, you feel it – it could be numbness, but it might also be anger or fear – you just surround it with the pause, the quiet, curious space that allows it to breathe a little inside you.

This creates the uplift and the transformation. It really is simple, but it does take an act of will – a small act of will. Although at times it may well feel like a big one!

As you journey deeper into the art of contemplation, I encourage you to be brave and look inside at your uncomfortable areas. Give yourself the space, time and commitment to explore them. That is when you will realise that inside those Shadows lie the Gifts, the treasures. But, few humans know to look for them there, because we have a tendency to distract ourselves away from pain.

Pivoting is a very powerful experience at the very heart of the art of contemplation, and as you move further into the practice, it will spread throughout your life. Here is another excerpt from 'The Art of Contemplation'.

The Reward of Pivoting – The Heart of Peace:

'Although it may seem to many like a romantic dream, pure love is the only lasting legacy we humans have. There is nothing comparable to it in all of creation. All our knowledge and science and self-importance falls away in the presence of such love. It is this love that we come from, and this love that we will return to. It is the fathomless mystery of the human heart. This pure love, though hard-earned and seldom witnessed on our earth, is the ultimate reward of the deeper reaches of contemplation. Those few who have embodied this love throughout history have found fewer words to describe it. They speak of it as an indescribable peace that resides in the human heart. It is this heart of peace that lies buried like a glittering gem inside each of us. It awaits the day when we will gather the courage to pierce our fear and softly allow the petals of our hearts to once again open fully.'

It is not just a dream. It is the only truth there is.

PIVOTAL BREAKTHROUGHS
THE ART OF CONTEMPLATION – PART 4

Pivoting is the turning point of our inner journey when we get to transform some deep, unseen shadow, some wounded part of our self. We transmute and change it into something higher, something positive, something creative and beautiful.

By creating more pauses in our life and therefore more inner space, we are making room in our life for pivotal moments, for this mysterious process of inner turning, where we pivot around a wound or a discomfort. The pearl in the oyster is created by a pivot around the ache, the problem, the grain of sand that the oyster cannot get rid of, so it builds a thing of beauty around it. It pivots around it, which is what we are also doing through the art of contemplation.

If you are already using the Gene Keys then you will have a good understanding of the language of the Spectrum of Consciousness and the Shadows, the Gifts and the Siddhis, which are the foundation of the Gene Keys. The experience of pivoting is the very knife edge of the Shadow transmuting into the Gift and releasing the aroma of the essence of the Siddhi. For example, the Shadow of the 15th Gene Key is Dullness, the Gift is Magnetism and the Siddhi is Florescence. For someone who is experiencing that Dullness – not necessarily the dullness of a day, but more like the inner being feeling dull, lacklustre, uninspired, unmotivated and adrift – rather than distracting yourself away from those feelings, you create space around them, and this can create the pivot.

You see that something in there, in the feeling – the discomfort and the ache – begins to reveal itself, and an energy shift takes place. It is something that takes place inside the body, in an embodied process. The energy shift releases the kinetic energy from the potential, and the potential energy becomes kinetic. In other words, it releases life force and vitality, which is why in this case it becomes Magnetism.

Then the mood shifts, the inner world shifts and the whole way which you look at life, at yourself and the world begins to shift, and you feel more positive, happier and lighter. That is how pivoting works. Then the Florescence means that the shift lives on in the world, because pivoting is a continuing experience. It is not just a moment, but a permanent cellular shift, and it goes on happening. Having done it once, it can easily happen again, and it gives you faith to keep on creating more space, more pauses, because the breakthroughs are so amazing!

I have had many pivotal experiences during my life. Many of them have taken place in my relationships with my children, my wife and my father. There is a particular one with my father that I remember, a sweet experience when I was younger. I had a real difficulty in my early twenties with my father because I couldn't get him to listen to me. I was having all these experiences of openings and expansions, and I was full of my spiritual journey, and I wanted him to know and understand it, but he wasn't very interested. He didn't speak the language and he couldn't relate to it. He was a gardener, and one of those gardeners who knew the Latin names of every plant.

I remember walking around the garden with him telling me the names of everything, and speaking Latin to me, and all of a sudden I just started to deeply relax and just enjoy his presence and his joy. And then I had a pivot, a complete emotional breakthrough. My heart opened and I let go of wanting him to understand me in that way and I just took him for what he was. I realised then that WAS him understanding me.

I allowed him into my heart, and I allowed the Latin in as well. It is just language, but underneath the language was joy, connection, intimacy. I felt that flow and he felt it too. We connected. After that afternoon, my relationship with my father was so much easier because I took all the pressure off him to be a certain way. I just let him be the way he wanted to be, and through that came our connection. Often we put pressure on people to listen in a certain way, and to speak our language when they don't want to, or they are not ready to. So we need to just let them speak their language because we will realise that underneath, the true language is of the heart.

I hope you can take this teaching of the art of contemplation into your life, and through creating pauses you can begin to watch the magic of the pivots. The pivots happen just occasionally, so you really remember them, and they can make wonderful stories, like the one with my father. I really recommend that when you have a pivotal breakthrough, you share it. Share it with your friends, and then you could also share it in the Gene Keys community. Share it because these moments are precious and they can give others breakthroughs. One person's pivot can become many people's. And although we can't consciously create a pivot, because it is out of our control, we can create a pause, and then something transformational occurs in us through those pauses. It is very simple and magical.

May you experience many, many pivotal moments.

MERGING
THE ART OF CONTEMPLATION – PART 5

Pausing, pivoting and merging are the three techniques that make up the art of contemplation. Merging grows out pivoting, and pivoting grows out of pausing, which is the key to the art of contemplation, and anyone can easily learn how to do it. If you are fortunate, a pivot will flow from the pause, and then merging flows from the pivots.

Merging is different from the other two because it is more like the backdrop and the deep, underlying reward and purpose of the art of contemplation. It could be said that pausing is the seed, pivoting is the flower and merging is the fruit. The fruit can't be rushed – it drops from the branch when it is ready. In the same way, merging happens in the background, although sometimes it can take years.

The art of contemplation ultimately opens us up to life in a much more profound way, which is why the third aspect is called merging, because we begin to merge with all that is. We experience a healthy sense of 'this is me' but also, *'I flow into all things. I trust all things. I am part of all things. I am part of the whole.'* Here is an excerpt from 'The Art of Contemplation'.

Merging:

'Merging involves moving deeper than ever into life, into the world, towards others. It is a state of flowering and an embracing of all facets of life. It is the threshold of our mastery. Merging is the heart of contemplation. Merging is an unflinching attitude we develop towards everything and everyone around us. No matter what happens, no matter what destiny brings us, we consciously move towards it, in a spirit of trust. We move to merge with it.

You cannot merge with something or someone unless you have already developed a vast open space within you. If you try and merge with a person without this inner space you will become entangled with them. This is a common story in human relationships. We become confused with the stories of others and they become confused with ours.'

It is really important to understand, especially in relationships, that when your story gets tangled up in someone else's story, and there are not enough pauses or space to disentangle all those dramas, we become trapped in the shadow patterns and the storylines, and we become entwined in a kind of tapestry. This kind of merging is called co-dependent merging, and it is unhealthy. It is healthy to the degree that it teaches us, but it is unhealthy because it constricts our love and our natural sense of being.

True merging happens as a conscious act of love and is the result of many pauses and many pivots. It is a maturing of our soul. It is a world view that grows in us. Again, from 'The Art of Contemplation':

'It is as though we have allowed our roots to spread into all the crevices of the world. There is nothing we try to escape from and no one whom we resent, envy or avoid.'

This may look as if we are losing our boundaries but it is actually the opposite. It is a paradox. We merge because we have become so centred and have such a polished sense of being, that it is safe for us to do so. The diamond of the self is opened on all sides so it can merge without losing its pure self, and the paradox is that the more it merges, the more beautiful and glittering the diamond becomes.

Many people fear that if they were to merge with the whole, they would lose themselves. But that is needless because when you have that polished gem of the self, the true self, it becomes more resplendent the more it opens. It is infinite and we are infinite beings in our capacity to merge with things, with life and with events.

There are three qualities – Generosity, Friendship and Gentleness – that create the environment for merging and they are all intimately linked. Generosity is about softening, opening and embracing things in a generous spirit. Sometimes it is unseen, so it can be very subtle. For example, someone wrongs you with an injustice, but instead of rushing to defend your honour, you soften, you open and you understand: '*Well, this has happened because there is something here for me that I can learn from.*' For the other person, you can treat them with respect and diplomacy in whatever way you need to. Whether you withdraw or whether you let them know that it wasn't OK with you, you do it in a respectful way.

The important thing is that you decide to learn from it. You are respectfully acknowledging what has come to you, looking for the learning in it and contemplating its deeper lesson. Perhaps it is inviting you to let go of something, something subtle. People usually expect a defence when they have launched an attack, but sometimes you can turn these situations around inside yourself and your response can be courteous rather than reactive, and that is generosity.

The second quality of friendship is very profound. For the Sufis, friendship is a way of life – they look at everything as their friend. Every act, situation, object or person is embraced as an opportunity to experience the inherent unity of all beings. Seeing everything as your friend has the effect of bringing the world closer to you. You enter into an intimacy with life and other people. If you offer friendship, it is unconditional. Even if they don't return your offer of friendship, it doesn't matter.

If they don't reciprocate or if they are not ready, that is part of your spaciousness. You just carry on with life, and you will be there waiting for when they do feel ready, even if they are never ready. Nonetheless, you extend that friendship in the spirit of generosity.

Gentleness, the third quality, is rooted in a Sanskrit term, *ahimsa*, which is a lovely word meaning harmlessness. This might come across as a bit weak, but actually it is a powerful discipline in non-violence. To be disciplined in *ahimsa* means that no thoughts, words or tones escape your aura with any edge to them, but, if they happen to, you can immediately take them back, learn from it and then forgive yourself. You are constantly refining the energy of gentleness as you are putting out the energy, and that is what creates the merging. It does not mean that you can't be really clear and one-pointed, but it means that even your one-pointedness has a polish. Even the edge has a kind of respect to it. Gentleness is rooted in dignity and self-respect, and you offer it to others and at the same time you offer it to yourself.

One of the hardest tasks in the art of contemplation is to be gentle with oneself, but it is the most important thing to remember. Make sure that you practice gentleness. Be easy on yourself and let yourself off the hook. Just like parenting a child, sometimes we have to parent ourselves in the same gentle way. And sometimes, when we are faced with violence, hatred or injustice, or someone behaving badly in some way, we have to remember that there is a wounded child in there. And how do you behave towards a wounded child? Yes, you have boundaries, but also you approach them in the spirit of gentleness because you know that is what a child needs. They have probably never really been loved, or they have forgotten what it is like to be loved.

So, along with boundaries and a sense of dignity, we treat all things with compassion, and that is the power of merging and the fruit of our contemplative practice. This brings us back to pausing. We must learn and remember how to pause. Increase pauses inwardly and outwardly in your life, and just allow the spaciousness of pausing to be fuelled by generosity of spirit, friendship and gentleness.

The world will consistently supply us with the means to polish our art of contemplation. It is doing so now and will continue to do so. One of the great gifts of being alive and in the body is that we get to move towards this mastery, which is the purpose of the art of contemplation.

THE DEEPER REACHES
OF CONTEMPLATION
THE ART OF CONTEMPLATION – PART 6

It takes time for truth to emerge out of the practice of contemplation, and time to really come down into the physical body. When it does come, it comes as an epiphany, which can happen in different ways for different people. It can come through tears, through an intense rush of truth, or it can come through a sort of deep explosion of joy or laughter. It is something that ripples through your body. It can come even through an illness, but the illness has a different quality to it, serving as a breakthrough that leaves you in a higher state as your body goes through a process of shedding a difficult memory pattern. It is actually being burnt from your DNA by the awareness that comes from contemplation.

There are three stages of breakthrough, three layers which can help us in understanding and coming to grips with our shadow patterns and our challenges in life. Allow is the first stage, Accept is the second, and Embrace is the third, where the deep core work is done in the cells of the body. Knowing which stage we are in can help to give us a sense of where we are in our emotional terrain, as well as where we are heading, and each stage helps us to surrender more deeply into the process.

The first technique of the art of contemplation is pausing, and it relates to the mind because it gives the mind space, which leads to insight. Pivoting, the second technique, gives space to the emotions, so that there can be an emotional breakthrough. Thirdly, the technique of merging leads to an epiphany, which is a cellular explosion, a transmutation, and is of the physical body.

Merging is a beautiful experience and it is where contemplation gives way to absorption, a higher state. Absorption is more of a mystical state, in which our body starts to secrete hormones through the pineal and pituitary glands, allowing us to access deeper states of wisdom that are ongoing.

We enter into these states at the higher reaches of contemplation. They do not take us out of the body, but take place deep within our body and our life. They can happen rhythmically in an infinite unfolding and merging, as we merge deeper and deeper into the field, into the different dimensions beyond time and space. The opening that contemplation leads to is endless and infinite. It is important to understand that there is no end to it because it is a constant, explosive journey of awakening through layers upon layers, over plateaus, hills and mountains, and which continues to open us from the inside out, like the petals of a flower.

After a while, contemplation becomes more than a habit, more than a technique, as it becomes deeply embedded in our nature and a part of who we are. It becomes mysterious in the sense that we are no longer doing the technique, but the technique is, almost, in a way, doing us. This is when the heart begins to really open up. We want to love and serve all, and not cause harm to anything.

One of the qualities that comes from merging is *ahimsa*, an ancient Indian principle of harmlessness. We give off an emanation of harmlessness because there is so much truth emerging through our being, and that one impulse of doing no harm overrides all others. This purity of heart sees its own essence in every creature, every person, every being and every thing, even in the shadow states.

As *ahimsa* burgeons in us, we start to see light even in the shadow states, and even within evil and corruption too. We begin to leave the game of revolution and empowerment, and we become blissful as we enter into a wider field where we see everything, even in its dark phases and its challenges, as conspiring to move towards the light.

Humour is the other thing that comes with this stage, and it comes from stepping out of the drama and realising that it is all just a game. It does not take away one iota from our empathy with those who are suffering, and, in fact, it surrounds and contains the suffering. Humour is a background awareness that doesn't have to be expressed, it just allows us to take life lightly, even when it is intense. It means we can surrender and let go into ever deeper levels and layers, and it is wonderful because, in a way, the humour is the crystallisation of divinity. You have moments when you think you understand something, but you don't. All your knowing is vaporised by the void, by the Great Mystery, and in that way the Great Teacher can always surprise you.

There is a nice story about Jesus after he resurrected. He comes back after that intense experience, and appears to the disciples for the first time, and the first thing he says is, *'Have you got anything to eat?'* It is a lovely moment, one of those that transcend understanding but give you an insight into truth, and the wonder of truth, and how it is hidden in unexpected places. Merging gives us openness in our being so that the unexpected can appear at any point, in any way.

This brings us back to pausing, as every pause that we take is an invitation, a possibility for greater merging. The pauses can be the tiniest moments, and the merging can be the tiniest things...

As I was communing with a beautiful sunrise one morning, I turned around and saw a beautiful little wild lily. It had a beautiful shape like a vagina, with a stamen inside it which looked quite phallic. It was looking towards the sun and I became entranced by it, and how it had shaped itself and grown there. I stared at it for what seemed like hours, contemplating it, as I and it basked in the sunrise. And I realised that it was me and I was it – that I was a representation of it, and I was there in another form, as the flower.

Contemplation can take us to the most unexpected places, where something mysterious opens up and we merge deeper and deeper with nature, with life and the events in our lives. The art of contemplation is the greatest teaching. If you keep exploring it, it can become the central and most important thing in your life. I hope it does.

TRAIN OF LIGHT

Running is a beautiful way to entertain the contemplative state, just like walking or anything that has a rhythmic quality.

One day I was running down an old, abandoned railway track which had several paths joining into it at different points along the track. It struck me that it was almost symbolic of the contemplative path, where you have a train of thought moving through you with different tributaries joining the main flow of thought at different moments. And when there is a break in the trees, you see the sunlight, and suddenly an insight drops in.

While I was running I was recalling a book I had been reading about Saint Thomas Aquinas's description of Christ's aura, his Body of Glory, the raiment of light and the energy signatures that he emitted. It seems that Saint Thomas went into a very deep contemplation for most of his life over the subject of the aura of the Master. What a great thing to contemplate.

Saint Thomas said that for the forty days prior to the resurrection, Christ's aura was expanding and expanding, and it was preparing him for the event of his crucifixion and resurrection and what was going to be a huge initiation.

Saint Thomas also said that Christ was able to expand and conceal the light from certain people at certain times so that it would not be too overpowering. So, when Christ was on Mount Tabor in his full glory and he fully released the resplendent light as the intelligence of God manifesting through his aura, his disciples fell on their faces.

I thought that Christ being able to conceal his light was a really powerful insight, and it powered and turbo-charged my contemplation while I was running. It opened up the almost cellular memories of the possibility of those Siddhic states for all of us to shine in.

Yogananda, who was an Indian Hindu monk, talks of a time when he ran to meet his master who had been away and was returning on the train. As Yogananda got to the station, he saw the train coming and shouted to one of the other disciples, *'The train is full of light. The whole train is filled with the light of the master.'* And as I was running, I thought of that train of light, the train of higher truth that I was running through.

 ## TWO CUPS

The drinking of tea can be a contemplative practice when it is done with mindfulness and awareness, and it can be wonderful for your inner cultivation. One of the disciplines I am learning is to take tea with me when I go out, so I can share it with somebody else. I love to drink fine, Chinese tea out of beautiful cups. So if I am heading out for a walk or to run errands, I like to take a beautifully prepared tea in a thermos with two cups, because when you can share your practice of tea drinking with others, it becomes a metaphor for life, for openness and for sharing your heart, your gifts and your authenticity. Whatever is coming through you can be shared with others, even personal or painful feelings.

So whenever you go out, always take two cups, not just one, because at any point life may bring you a potential new friend. Something unexpected could come to you, a person, a creature, or a change of plan as you are moving on your trajectory for the day. You may find yourself in a gap, or stopped in your tracks by something or someone, and that is an opportunity, a pause, an in-breath, and the potential for a cup of tea with someone. So when there is an opportunity, say hello, take out the second cup, invite them to share your tea and pour the tea for two. What is this new, unexpected experience, and what might it bring? What gifts might come with it? Take time to explore it and savour it, be gentle and open. I hope you are understanding this metaphor.

There are many ways in which life will try to engage us. If we are learning the art of contemplation, then we are also learning how to pause and listen to life.

That is how we let life in, and that is how life then starts to do its magic, when we are open to it. But we have to have enough of a sense of core stability to be open to responding to the unexpected, and to allow life to choreograph our destiny, rather than being the person setting out to achieve x and y every day and doing all the hard work. This might be a strategy for success in the outer world, but it isn't a strategy for success in your inner life.

Your inner life has to be open to the ebbs and flows of fate, of dharma. So as life comes to you and offers you something, you need to give that something your time, even if only a little bit of your time.

Do you recall the people who wait on the street with clipboards, who want to talk to you and sign you up to something, but you are always in a rush to get somewhere and want to get past them and avoid looking them in the eye? You might even move to the other side of the street so that you don't have to talk to them. But what you could do is look them in the eye and offer a moment of recognition, and tell them, *'Thanks. But I really can't talk to you today. One day I might, but I'm not able to now, sorry.'*

In this way, you acknowledge them, validate them and in that moment you have opened to life instead of closing to it, but you have also kept to what is correct for you. One day you may slide into a pause and find that you have a spare couple of minutes just to give them the gift of someone listening. You are not necessarily there for what they want to tell you and most likely you are not interested in what they are offering. But give them the two minutes anyway. It can be a magical thing.

So, take two cups wherever you go, and then you create an opening in your aura that will open more and more. And life will keep bringing you friends, all kinds of new friends, and those friends will open up connections and fractal lines to all kinds of possibilities and miracles that you would otherwise have been missing. Practice this art of tea, and whenever you go out, remember to always take a second cup.

FRAGMENTS OF LIGHT
CHAPTER 4

A NEW FUTURE

*As this current age ends and we prepare the
ground for the new epoch and the generations
to come, we might wonder what the
future holds for us as a species.*

*The new paradigm is on the horizon, and what is
coming is nothing less than a beautifully upgraded
version of humanity with a vastly heightened
sensitivity and awareness, and a magical and
radically new way of being.*

 # TRETA YUGA

The next epoch, known as the Treta Yuga, is part of an ancient model of the evolution of Gaia and of humanity which originates from ancient Indian religious texts called the Vedas. It works through four great epochs or cycles, known as *yugas*, which have been mathematically calculated and revised in many ways.

Essentially, we begin in perfection, which we then fall from in a great arc, letting go gradually and forgetting more and more until we are at the bottom, at the base, where we have fallen completely into the material world, and are completely separate from our spiritual origins. And although heaven and earth are a long way apart, we then begin to ascend again. The current rises, remembering itself as it climbs to the top, when we have a gradual synthesising of the material and the spiritual, the above and below.

The happy ending is that we arrive back where we began but we are richer through the journey. It is the Arc of the Aeons, and is a wonderful riddle.

The model that I have found most useful is the one by Sri Yukteswar, a great sage. He postulated that the nadir, the base, where we sank to the deepest part, known as the Kali Yuga, was around 500 AD, which is the Dark Ages, and after that point we began to move up again, and we have been ascending ever since. The process is really interesting when you get into the nitty gritty, because in each yuga are sub-yugas of the whole map, almost like a hologram, and then each one of them again is a sub-sub-yuga. You can really see the patterns within the patterns.

It used to be that we were aware of the magic of life, the magical connection between all things, where matter and spirit were combined. We were a bit of both, and so we were able to manipulate matter in different ways and were more merged with the field of consciousness. Slowly as we came down on the Arc, we forgot the magic and lost track of it, until we sank into the material world and forgot our divine origins entirely. The descent was about forgetting, about coming from a magical world and then forgetting that world, and those magical practices becoming solidified or hardened. That is what happened in many great religious practices, which were initially of the magical reality, but became increasingly ritualised until they were empty, because we had forgotten the magical world.

We are now beginning the ascent in something called the ascending Dwapara Yuga, as opposed to its descending stage. Coming up from the base is about the ascent back to the magical through the material. We have to rise up through mastering the material realm, which is where science comes in, and a different pattern of ascension. In the Dwapara Yuga, where we are now, we are remembering and understanding the material plane more and more. The next stage is the Treta Yuga, which will come in a couple of thousand years from now, and will last for many thousands of years.

I was trying to envisage that future, where we will remember more of ourselves, when I was out running one day. I happened to be on a golf course at the time, and it got me thinking back to when I was younger and quite a good golfer. Those outside it may find golf hard to appreciate, but it is a really contemplative sport, because it is just you alone, your swing, your rhythm, the ball and the hole – that's it. It is all down to you, and there is a purity to that.

The rhythm of your swing is an unconscious thing and when you are in harmony, it is the sweetest feeling when you connect with the ball. To be a master of any sport you have to practice it over and over again until that sweet spot has become ingrained in you. But in the Treta Yuga, I saw that every shot you took would be in the sweet spot because it would be in harmony with the Tao. Imagine you got a hole-in-one every time. It would be regarded as a miracle, with every shot taken in harmony with all that is, and the game would be no longer a game. You could never lose. It would be like those wonderful films where great martial artists end up conspiring together because they are so equal in their mastery that neither can win.

You could also apply this to running, which is another thing that I love to do. Imagine you are in an immortal body. You would be able to run for weeks without stopping or tiring because your energy field would be connecting to the quantum realm and drawing its sustenance from it. The joy of the run itself would nourish you. There would be an endless pulsing rhythm and flow, and you would be able to run and run, and be in ecstatic bliss forever.

Think about a football team, in the consciousness together – the perfection of the passing, the movement, the rhythm, the flow, the positioning of each player, in perfect synchronisation with the whole. They would be unbeatable, and boring to play against because every time you tried to find a weak spot the team would automatically shift into another unbeatable sequence.

You might think of swimming. In the Treta Yuga, you would be able to hold your breath underwater indefinitely, just drawing breath from your inner core, from the deep pulse coming from inside you. You could swim with the whales and dolphins, and glide down to great depths with your organs able to adjust to the immense pressure.

In the Treta Yuga, if you sat down to play the piano and thought of someone you love, you would start to play the music of their soul. It would emerge through the consciousness field, and out through your hands because of your great love. I imagine many musicians will have experienced that. In the Treta Yuga, you would not have to become a musician or even practice because in the consciousness field, mastery would be interchangeable. You could sit down never having played the piano and through your love and the soul of the one you love coming through your hands, you would make the greatest music.

With architecture, the architect would go out into the landscape, look at it and see the perfect building that has grown out of the landscape and is already there, in its wholeness. The architect would simply recreate that in the material realm because the imprint of it is there. They would see it in perfect harmony with that particular piece of the landscape and its energies. It would be a place of pure harmony and beauty.

Think about sculpture and the uncarved block. The sculptor would take a block of wood or stone, and through their love the shape would materialise as they remove what is not needed, to reveal the sculpture within. This would not be the domain of just a few masters but everyone ascending into this higher consciousness.

I want to encourage this kind of thinking. It broadens horizons, expanding the sense of boundlessness and of what is possible. We are in a different yuga right now, but to know where we are going gives a great perspective on where we are. It lightens the load in some way to know that is what we truly are.

We are magical beings, and step by step we are going to remember that. We are going to regain those heightened states, those natural states in which the material and the spiritual come together, and we will perfect the physical plane, we will perfect ourselves and our world, and we will perfect our soul. That is the purpose of being here – for the perfecting of our souls and the perfecting of all that is around us.

THE RETURN OF MAGIC

In March 2018, Pluto began an important long-term planetary transit when it moved into the 61st Gene Key of inner truth, the Siddhi of Sanctity. This particular transit was especially magical as it has been about 250 years since Pluto last made this transit, since the end of the Age of Enlightenment, before the Industrial Revolution, when the Earth was, in a way, still untarnished.

The transit has been a long one, giving several years of being able to play in the 61st Gene Key, until November 2022. It was a powerful and significant transit for us as a species, as it signified the Return of Magic, the magical forces of the earth, of Gaia.

The 61st Gene Key is part of the *Ring of Gaia*, and Pluto's transition through it brought in something completely new and extraordinary. However, not everyone may experience this, as it is a sensitive, subtle, dynamic field. And when I use the word magic, some might think I'm a bit 'alternative', but, for me, magic is a tangible essence. It is a quintessence and it is all around us. It is like 'the Force' as it connects us through its field.

For a long time, humanity lost touch with magic. We forgot about magic, and it became dormant. We could contact the magic only in certain special places, out in unspoilt nature, at the right time of year, when the moon was right, or at the right time of day when the forces were available. But now the magic is returning, and it has returned in a cycle that is going to take us somewhere extraordinary, because it is the seeding of a new kind of future for humanity.

For those of us who are sensitive, this is our time, because the magical forces are now available to us for the first time in a long while. They are reawakening, and we will have a new relationship with them. Not a relationship in which we worship them as gods, as we have done, but a symbiosis, a process in which we help each other. Because these forces, deities that live in the earth, are part of us. They are not separate from us. They are part of our extended being, our extended expansion of consciousness. As we reach out and touch these beings, we can create relationships with them, we can work together, because they have powers that we do not possess, in realms that we cannot yet see. There are wormholes in the dimensions of reality that enable these beings to take shortcuts for us, and they can bring things to fruition much more quickly than we can on the material plane.

It is a time of immense power and we must handle it carefully, because it is very easy to be overwhelmed by the high frequencies. Many people have fallen into that trap or are simply not pure enough in their heart to hold true. Some carry too much self-interest, and when they use the magic, it pollutes them in some way and they become tarnished, though it is not the magic that causes that. But it becomes a darker kind of magic and then, invariably, it collapses in on itself. It is noteworthy that the Shadow of the 61st Gene Key is Psychosis.

So, it is vital that we are clear and open, and that we do the necessary work in our relationships, in our Venus work, and our core-stability work, as we have to be ready to meet this magic as it returns, as it will continue to imprint us all for generations to come.

It is a very exciting time. So, go! Get out into the field where the magic lives.

THE EYE OF THE NEEDLE
GENE KEY 19 – PART 1

One morning, I received some mystical, prophetic transmissions, and I found myself spontaneously travelling into the Gene Keys Synthesis and into the 19th Gene Key. As I was contemplating this Gene Key, I started to ponder the Great Change that we are moving though right now, which is connected to it.

The founder of the Human Design system, Ra Uru Hu, had a profound insight that there would be a split in a place in our genetics between, in Human Design terms, the 19th gate and the 49th gate. The 49th Gene Key is related in its Codon Ring, to the 55th Gene Key which is about Freedom, and is central to the Great Change. Ra predicted that there would be a division in the 19-49 channel that would shake our whole species. It is a channel in our bio-circuitry which connects the 19th and 49th gates, and it relates to many things, but ultimately to our ancestry, and our relationship to resources. And it is not just referring to basic resources that keep us alive in the physical form, but spiritual and emotional resources and needs as well – the need to be touched, to reach out, to be supported and be part of what it is to be human and to know that you are connected to others.

The Shadow of the 19th Gene Key is Co-Dependence, which is essentially about the fear of lack. It is what drives the whole shadow frequency – that we don't have enough resources. We are driven by a deep fear of lack and scarcity which can make us become aggressive, and sometimes it can make us kill, which, as we know, is part of our ancestral story. We kill to hold on to territory, and we kill animals because we want to eat them to survive. Our civilisation is driven primarily by this fear of lack. It creates competition between tribes and between nations, between all of us.

When the chips are down and there is a question of survival, fear comes to the surface. Divisions become even stronger and fear moves through the gene pool like a virus. But there is something changing in our DNA around that fear, and we are being given the opportunity to transcend it, and this means that we will have to transcend some really basic human instincts that we have always connected to, one of those being touch.

The Gift of the 19th Gene Key is Sensitivity. Higher sensitivity is where we reach out and touch, not just with our hands but through our energy body, through our higher dimensional body. So we can touch dimensions that we have never touched before as we reach out to the higher expanses of this Gene Key. This removes the need for physical touch because of the higher version of touch available – the aura touch.

When you sit within the field of a teacher, or a great master, you sit in what is called *satsang*. You don't need to touch the master because being in the field is enough. That is the higher touch, and it breaks the need for co-dependence, because that higher touch feeds at a much deeper level. It allows us to transcend many things, the need for attention from others, the need to love, and, ultimately, the need to be loved .

In the Dream Arc, which is a Gene Keys programme where we ascribe different creatures to each Key and so add more layers of archetypal insight, the 19th Gene Key is represented by the camel. This got me thinking and I pondered on the idea of the camel, and the saying of Christ, *'It is easier for a camel to enter through the eye of the needle, than it is for a rich man to enter the kingdom of heaven.'* It is a mysterious idea and one which many have pondered.

I see the eye of the needle as a tiny little hole, a wormhole at the core of our being which we have to pass through. It is actually at the core of every cell of our being, but its physical location is in the belly, in the belly button. It is the tiniest, infinitesimal point. We have to pass through that wormhole and when we do, if we can, we discover unlimited superabundant resources of joy and light, and a superabundance of being. We have to move through a lot of shadow stuff to get to that point, but that is the journey, and if you are scrabbling around on the surface trying to gather resources out of a fear of lack, then you are building up resources from that place of fear.

Whether we are doing it addictively because we want to accumulate more and more, or whether we are genuinely hungry, we have a craving and a need to feed the physical. Yet there is a higher potential inside us, that we can be fed by other sources, so that one day we will be able to thrive through energy alone.

The shift is taking place in the 19th Gene Key, and we are changing as a species. A break is occurring, a splitting in our DNA, which is creating a new architecture, a new kind of human being. This is linked to the 55th and the 59th Gene Keys, which are also where this huge shift is occurring.

The 55th Gene Key is about Freedom, and the 59th Gene Key is about Intimacy. So you come to the notion of touch here because, as the light, the radiance and the superabundant energy that pours through us, are released into our aura, the need for physical intimacy changes. There is a higher form of intimacy coming that will not require physical touch, and will be ultimately far richer without.

There is a wonderful professional freediver called Tanya Streeter. She often swims with wild creatures and is an amazing sort of mermaid. Talking about her experience of swimming with whale sharks, she said that you must never break the touch barrier with them, because if you do you will have almost broken that higher sensitivity where you are connected. In the same way, people who go for a swimming with dolphins experience will often want to reach out and try to touch the dolphins. But unless the creature comes to you, you should never break the touch barrier, because there is a kind of subtle stream of communication that takes place without touch.

I am a modern human and I love touch and physicality, but there is a higher-dimensional human coming online. It is interesting that this is the way that our species is going. Although we have a physical need for touch, the internet has changed things and there are not so many opportunities for touch now. Even when we were self-isolating, we became accustomed to it, in a way. It all contributes to the splitting that is taking place in our species, through opening up the potential for a higher form of touch.

So we have to go in through that eye of the needle. We have to go inward, deep into our being, which takes courage because we have to let go of all of the distractions that are out there. We are always looking for the answer outside ourselves, in people, science, love and relationships. We go searching for answers, while the answer is inside us. For millennia, sages have been saying that the answer is within. So when we pass through that eye of the needle inside us we will discover ultimate abundance.

The relationships of the future are going to look very different, because they will not require physical touch. They will have physical touch and celebrate it, but the highest form of freedom will be to travel outside one's body with one's awareness.

We will realise that we are far more than physical beings, we are interdimensional beings, and our awareness can not only take us to the furthest reaches, but also right into the core of another being. To be that transparent, to be right inside another person's being at every level without the need for physical touch, is a level of intimacy that most of us cannot even envisage.

It is not that there will be no physical touch, but a transcendence is coming and it will open up a new era for us. As we move towards that, there will be differences in how we react to it. There will be those who react out of the fear of scarcity and lack and use the old survival strategies, and those who will move with the new energies, going within to find the deep resources inside. Then they will connect with others and, instead of building bunkers, we will build communities. We will build heart streams that connect us, to find a higher level of support and nourishment, instead of segregating ourselves into little fear bunkers based on survival.

Ultimately, in the higher reaches of the 19th Gene Key, the Siddhi is Sacrifice. We have to sacrifice our fear of death. We have to sacrifice the illusion that this is all there is. Knowing that we are an eternal being will allow us to transcend all those physical needs that keep the body alive. At the highest level, it does not even matter if the body dies. Survival is less important than connection to others, and less important than love. There is no 'death', because we transcend it.

PLANET OF SACRIFICE
GENE KEY 19 – PART 2

The 19th, 60th and 61st Gene Keys, known collectively as the *Ring of Gaia*, are a part of the mysterious teachings of the Gene Keys called the Codon Rings. The *Ring of Gaia* holds many secrets, but particularly secrets around the Earth and its transformation. The 19th Gene Key, especially, is about transmuting, which happens through sacrifice, primarily through us and our lives. Sacrifice, the 19th Gene Key's Siddhi, its highest component, is a word that many of us are uncomfortable with, and yet we live on a planet where sacrifice is a constant process.

The whole nature of life is to sacrifice itself for something higher to evolve. It is what we do. The highest form of sacrifice is to sacrifice what is lower for what is higher, and what is pure. We sacrifice our lower desires on the altar of our freedom, and receive the reward. This is how it plays out. Every creature is bound up in this drama of sacrifice. At this stage of our evolution, we have been asked in recent times to sacrifice our personal freedoms and wishes for the sake of the whole and for the vulnerable. It is an interesting parallel that Covid-19 has the number 19, and that Sacrifice is the Siddhi of Gene Key 19. There are no mistakes in these things.

The three Siddhis of the Gene Keys in the *Ring of Gaia*, the 19th Siddhi of Sacrifice, the 60th Siddhi of Justice and the 61st Siddhi of Sanctity, play in concert together, and are deeply mysterious. As the form of the 60th Siddhi sacrifices itself, a new form, the inner truth of the 61st Siddhi, shines through. With every sacrifice that we make another layer of inner truth is revealed to us. We start to hear in more and more subtle dimensions; we see more and we become more.

The Gift of the 19th Gene Key is Sensitivity, and human beings are changing and evolving. Our DNA, our instrumentation is opening up higher faculties to tune in to the etheric world, which is the subtle world of dimensions that exists behind all things, and we realise that we are connected to all beings through the etheric dimension. Gaia is alive with subtle presences, and has many layers of sensitivity. Every creature, every plant, every sound and every colour has a divine presence, a specific higher, subtle presence, and everything is surrendering itself for the benefit of the whole. This is the game of life, death and rebirth. This is our planet – the planet of sacrifice.

To truly understand the meaning of sacrifice, we each need to contemplate it for ourselves and embody what it means. Life will regularly bring us opportunities to sacrifice an old view for a new view, an old paradigm for a higher paradigm. This is what opens us up to the higher, divine currents. When we surrender to a higher impulse and let go of something that previously we did not want to part with, we receive something in recompense and it opens and expands us.

Consider this in your life, and consider each day what you could choose to sacrifice. It could just be a bad word about someone or something that you might have said, but you stop yourself, and instead decide to offer it up by choosing not to. That tiny sacrifice is what brings the gift, the beauty and the pure reward. We sacrifice the lower to something higher, and for every sacrifice there is a karmic reward. Divine justice comes into play. This is something that is opening up in humanity, and something to go into deeply. To make these sacrifices willingly on behalf of the whole, so that we break our co-dependence and come into true interdependence, is truly noble.

MAGICAL THINKING
GENE KEY 19 – PART 3

The teaching of the 19th Gene Key is about a deep spiritual need to worship something beyond ourselves, but at this time of the Great Change, Gene Key 19 is changing and mutating. This change is happening in the body, and part of the teaching is rooted in Human Design knowledge, and in the Human Design Bodygraph. The shift is occurring in the DNA of all humans, and because everything in the cosmos is interconnected it is changing at all levels throughout creation because there are no isolated changes or mutations. They do not exist. A great change is a change throughout the chain of the cosmos, and humans are just one small part of it.

Sensitivity is the Gift of this Gene Key, a sensitivity to the transdimensional realities, and as we awaken as a species, we are awakening to all the different dimensions and layers. Our new awareness centres open up, and the solar plexus, especially, truly opens up our potential as a species to live a cosmic interdimensional life, because of the shift in our DNA and in our awareness. This shift in the 19th Gene Key is from worship to embodiment, and it is why our old religions, the tribal religions that are based on worship are declining and falling away, and a new paradigm is emerging.

I believe that the first human religions began with the 19th Gene Key. The Tungus people in Siberia believe that their ancient shamanic religion was one of the first primal religions, and interestingly the word shaman may have originated from the Tungusic language. In the modern age, we have tended to look upon the indigenous belief systems as less evolved intellectually than ours because of the way that they use magical thinking, and view life and the universe through a magical lens, which we see as superstitious. We project onto them that they have superstitions and rituals that we don't, while we have grown and evolved beyond that. Yet now we can honour our ancestors and indigenous peoples by integrating their views into a modern holistic, transcendent whole. And fortunately many of the old ways have been kept alive by our indigenous peoples.

In Ken Wilber's system of Integral Theory, his colour-coded scale 'Altitudes of Human Development', shows magical thinking and superstition at the lower levels of primal religion, and represented by magenta. Near the top of the scale, teal and turquoise represent the higher ways of viewing, and the higher interdimensional mind. The beautiful thing is that we can include a way of looking at the cosmos that is rooted in the earth, in our ancestors and in indigenous tribes even today, and integrate it in our new spiritual paradigm. We do not leave it behind and move on to some other view. Instead we integrate it, transcend it and include it, and this is very powerful. The Tibetans have done this in how they integrated their shamanic Bon tradition into their Buddhist tradition. They have ended up with a very colourful, tantric version of Buddhism that is alive and vibrant, and filled with deities and rituals.

In this new view we can integrate all world views, not just the Buddhist, and this is where the 19th Gene Key comes in. This transition is really important. I call it the art of magical thinking because it looks at the universe through magical eyes. This could be misunderstood, but there is a distinct difference between fantasy and delusion, and magical thinking. Magical thinking means being able to use the right brain and the creative imagination, while at the same time using our intuition to guide us. So we allow ourselves to think like a child, but we do it objectively. This is the essential difference, because in the times of the old superstitions we identified with the magical universe and became entangled with it. With the new view, we don't identify with it, and instead use the creative imagination in a magical way, integrating it into a higher aspect.

So we draw from the Eastern tradition, such as the unity consciousness and non-dual perspectives, but we also bring in another aspect of the right brain, which is playfulness, and we find that we can play in the magical universe. This approach works well with the creative impulse, whereas some very pure non-dual traditions do not really absorb it. They are not creative because they come from the Eastern mindset, and they are very pure in that sense. But when you bring in the Western world as well, you have an amazing confluence of all the archetypes that are built into that, so you end up with a completely different spirituality, a rich and playful one.

Human beings are just one chain of evolution, and there are many parallel evolutions. The Devic evolution is a subtle layer of life force that surrounds all living creatures and all beings on our planet. And interacting with animals, birds, insects, plants, crystals, stones, the elements, the stars and everything, is the inner world and the playground of the shaman. Theirs is the true magic of using the art of correspondences, seeing the connections between everything, and gaining great illumination through that as a spiritual path. They enter the underworld, the psychotropic realm, to look for insights, and then weave it all together. The 19th Gene Key brings this shamanic path alive and the shift in it propels us into a new kind of spirituality.

Many Devic dimensions and etheric realms exist in the etheric plane. Of the five elements, earth, water, fire, air and ether (or *aether*), ether is the fifth element and the transcendent one.

Ether is the essence which allows us to interact between the etheric dimensions and realms such as the elf realm. J.R.R Tolkien famously wrote in great detail about elves, and even created an entire Elvish language in 'The Lord of the Rings', and there are many other wonderful fantasy books with whole worlds and languages that we believe were created in the author's imagination. Another way of looking at it is that those epic fantasy stories with their Elvish names, details and language already existed in the Devic dimension, and are actually a history of the elf realm. Someone who had that cross-species gate of the 19th Gene Key in their profile would be able to transcribe such things, thinking it was coming from their imagination, and it does. But what if it were actually real? What if fantasy is reality? What if fantasy and reality are merged?

The art of magical thinking is where fantasy and reality come together, and it is very subtle. The elf world (I can't quite believe that I'm talking about the elf world!) exists in a subtle dimension that generally we can't see, but it has a parallel evolution to the human world. Some people might be able to see it at the times of crossover, when the portals between the realms open up, particularly between the human and Deva realms. This opening and closing of the portals between the realms is often dictated by the cycles of the moon as it waxes and wanes, and it is how those who know magic or wicca use the crossing-over points to bring information back and forth.

Time is the key. Essentially there are parallel evolutions that exist in different time realms from us. The elf beings, that we humanise and call elves, exist in a version of time that is different from ours. The elemental beings and nature spirits of the Deva realm are relatively immortal compared to us, because their version of time is so different.

The lifespan of human beings is now approaching a hundred years, but this is very short compared to the Deva realm. There are legends of elves and humans falling in love, but because the human lifespan is so short and the elf one so long, there is also great longing and sadness woven between our realms. These stories, myths and traditions emerge from the crossing-over points and those who cross over.

Sometimes, elvic or devic beings incarnate, or half-incarnate into humans. One half is in the Deva realm, and the other in this world. This is magical thinking, and it is a rich playground that opens up boundless possibilities for understanding the subtle realms. The 19th Gene Key understands the subtle realms, but you have to think in a different way and enter into the realm of fantasy while being aware that it is not necessarily fantasy. Because reality and fantasy are interconnected in a way that we cannot yet understand.

In the wider interdimensional mind there is no original thought, because everything already exists. Our imagination does not invent anything, and whatever we think we have invented already exists in some other form. We bring it into the human realm, and the level of our genius is in how open we are to the subtle dimensions and to the Causal Plane. We can open up a whole realm of magical thinking and begin to penetrate the other realms using the power of our creative imagination, and transfer information across the threshold of these parallel evolutions.

There are mystical places where portals to the subtle realms open at certain times. The memory of the places and times are encoded in the place, in sanctuaries or stones. If we are thinking magically, we can be drawn to those places at such times and unlock some of their secrets.

The ultimate spiritual journey is to bring together different spiritual modalities and paths. Combining the purity of the non-dual perspective of the deep Eastern paths of Buddhism, such as Advaita, with the wealth of the creative imagination creates a new paradigm, a new spiritual realm, which is infinite in terms of its adventures. This is why we should not fall for the mistake of thinking that incarnation is an error that we have fallen into and must escape from. We think that we have to free ourselves from the Maya and the illusion, but actually we should be playing in it. We have to become awake and then we can play in it. Becoming awake and then leaving for some higher dimension is not the path of the future. Playing in it and exploring the realms is the way. We are here to explore.

We are journeyers, eternal voyagers of consciousness. Each of us is a separate soul within the panoply of multiple souls, but we are all one. We are also creators, gods and goddesses. This is where magical thinking from the ancestors suddenly comes alive again within this new framework, and then we can honour them, instead of pushing them aside in the manner of the old ways. The old ways are very powerful; they have to be brought forward now, understood, and then woven into a new paradigm.

This is the magic of the 19th Gene Key, and in the Siddhi of Sacrifice we have to let go of the old and the new ways, in order to merge them and bring them all into a new world. This new way of being has freedom at the core – the freedom to explore and to move on from narrow principles such as, 'This is how it has to be. Keep things pure. Have only one lineage and stay with it.' Because the new way is through understanding that all lineages have one source, like a rainbow with the colours of all the lineages cross-connecting and cross-pollinating.

This is all a playground that we can explore, but we should not get lost in it. That will be the key, and the reason that we have to do our groundwork. You have to deal with your emotional wounds, negative thinking, self-worth issues – all your suffering. You have to deal with it all, and then you will be ready to play in the wider field, otherwise you cannot do it. That is why I have laid out all the groundwork in the Gene Keys, and as the path of the Gene Keys unfolds, the higher, magical realms come later, after the wound work and the shadow work, because they are on a higher path.

The *Ring of Gaia*, the codon ring that contains the 19th Gene Key, contains all the hidden secrets, and they are cracking and opening now. But the groundwork has to be done before you can move to the higher level, otherwise you can get fixated on magical thinking. This is my caution, because I have opened up this box, this chest of marvels, and I have seen many New Age people lost down these corridors of fantasy. If you have not prepared yourself by doing your inner work, in your body, in your health, in your relationships, then you have no business being in these magical realms, and you will get lost and not unlock the true power. You will not be able to flourish, your health will always forestall you, and you will find that prosperity and abundance do not come to you.

So you must be prepared, and in the Gene Keys this means doing the Golden Path, which is a transformational route through your Hologenetic Profile. In there are all the teachings that you need in order to clear the way, so that magical thinking can be put to good use. Just do not be tempted to go into the magical realms too soon. But the invitation is there to explore them and play with them as and when the time is right.

This magical 19th Gene Key is changing us and it will open up new pathways and a whole new spirituality filled with adventure, boundless light and possibility. Once again humanity can be an innocent child running through the meadows of life, exploring and opening up the treasure chests the creative imagination holds.

So, make sure you do your groundwork because there is a joyous, beautiful time coming our way.

QUANTUM CONSCIOUSNESS

Humanity is at a turning point. We are mutating a new awareness which is opening up inside us in the solar plexus, in our core, down in the belly. Our digestive system is part of the old primal design from when we were creatures with tails living on the horizontal, and for us now it is quite inefficient. But as our world changes, we change and adapt with it, and our diet adapts too. Nowadays, because our hearts are not open, we can tend to eat a lot. But when we fall in love, the opposite happens, our solar plexus opens up, our heart centre opens and we cannot eat. This is what love can do.

In the old system of chakras from the Vedic tradition, there is a huge quantum leap from the third chakra, the *manipura*, to the fourth, the *anahata*, which is from the belly, the solar plexus to the heart. With the new solar plexus mutation and the new awareness that is arising, the heart opens up, and it opens up permanently. And we don't just fall in love with another person, we experience that level of intensity with the whole, because love is our resonance with the quantum field of life. When we open up our hearts and we love everything and everyone, we become love. People have accessed this state of being since the beginning of time, and it is so alluring to us because it carries the future mutation inside it.

Quantum consciousness really opens us up from the solar plexus – most of the embodiment process that we teach in the Gene Keys is rooted in the mutation in the solar plexus. So, as a global community in the world, for us to move into collective awareness, we are going to have to go deeper and deeper into our bellies.

It will take some time and surrender, and some courage and tenderness, because of all the layers of karma, wounding, memory and discomfort that are rooted and imprinted in the cellular DNA of our gut that have always been in there. That is why the Vedic Rishis, the Taoists and the shamanic indigenous cultures all around the world made the belly the center of their training. They saw the navel as the beginning and the end, the *omphalós*, the *ouroboros*, the *dantian*, the cauldron, the Grail. It is always the belly.

It has been discovered through the genetic sequencing of intestinal flora that there is a hundred times more DNA in the gut than in the rest of the body put together. It is all bacteria and it represents a vast awareness system. Every one of those tiny single-celled organisms has the potential for a rudimentary awareness. They are practically identical from body to body, and they function inside us like universal holographic hardware that meshes us together and connecting us, that is their potential.

All that DNA, the bacteria that is our intestinal flora is responsive to us, to our thoughts, feelings and intent, our dreams and our words. It is super-sensitive. Our awareness is the software and if we program it in a high enough frequency, all that life inside us lights up. It lights up as in traditional Hindu and Vedic paintings which show the chakras and the light radiating from people's bodies, and it could be that the light is generated by microscopic bacteria.

Bacteria are the most ancient, mysterious and super-conductive life form in our ecosphere. They have the ability to trap light and emanate it through phosphorescence. The tiniest organisms often hold the biggest surprises. Place your hand on your belly and think about that.

The journey of the Gene Keys is a process of alchemy. It is about moving into our Shadows, those pain points inside us, with awareness, and processing what is inside. As the memory is released, over time the heart begins to open wider and wider into the Gift frequency, and then the Siddhi. That is the Gene Keys journey in a nutshell. It is awakening group consciousness, quantum consciousness and a higher awareness. It is all about connection, opening up, cooperation and coordination, group synergy and, ultimately, communion. We experience that as limitless and unconditional love, and as joy. It is all inside us waiting to be released, but we have to do some alchemy first.

So, give your belly some attention. Hold your hand there. Just allow whatever comes to come, and give it some love. Give yourself some love, and in time, you will open up.

THE BIG QUESTION

There is a universal question, a simple question about the world around us that appears to be in decay. For the most part, our leaders are not working together, and the Earth and its creatures are paying the price. This message is not being taken seriously enough. When we look at the outer world we see wars and many other huge problems. Maybe it has always been like that. But, in fact, on one level, our world is in a better shape than it ever has been, yet on another level it seems also to be in decline. Those of us who are sensitive and are looking at it through eyes of clarity realise that we cannot continue like this because it is unsustainable and we are heading towards a precipice. So what can we do? What can I do? That is the big question.

What one has to understand is that there are two currents at work. There is the current that we see in the outer world, and there is the current that we see or experience in the inner world. If you are operating only in the outer world, you will not even know about the inner current. Many people do not know what the inner world is or that there even is an inner world. But there are things to be discovered, the wisdom and the truth that are inside us, and a whole inner journey to explore. Looking at the outer world it may seem that things are worsening and we are heading for the threshold of a crisis, and if that is where your focus is, it can be depressing. So you have to balance that with the inner world and your inner work. The inner world is going the opposite way and is a different experience. There is a light emerging and huge opportunities for growth, expansion, evolution and the opening up of possibilities.

If you are not meditating, not looking within and not experiencing the magic of the inner world, you may not know what I am talking about. But if you do, then you will feel these currents of light, and you will feel the possibilities, perhaps in a way that you have never felt before.

What we need to do is strengthen our connection to the inner world more and more, because out of that inner connection come the clarity and understanding of what to do on the outside. We cannot do it the other way around, by looking at the problem and all its manifestations, and trying to deal with it from there. We have to work on our own suffering and transmute what is inside us. So we have to go deep inside to the core of our being, and work there.

If we focus on rebuilding our inner clarity and improving our inner self-esteem, our wisdom, love and connection to compassion, then out of that will come the clarity of knowing what to do on the outside, if anything. This depends very much on what is our inner direction, our dharma, our alignment to the universal or divine will, which we have to feel, but that can only happen when we are connected on the inside.

So to answer the question, 'What can I do?' Make those connections on the inside, deepen them, strengthen them, do the inner work and move through the transformation of your consciousness. If you shift the low-frequency victim patterns that are embedded inside you to a higher level, then your heart begins to open, you begin to trust and move into forgiveness. You connect with the universal wisdom, while moving into deeper and deeper levels of detachment from the outer world, as you start to sink into a state of deep trust. You realise that every single moment of life is taken care of, not by you but by a universal hand that is at work behind everything, doing only what is good for the whole, as that is all it knows. Even when things move into terrible crisis, strife, deep suffering and darkness, it is for the sake of the whole, in order that something can awaken through that darkness.

Every one of us who has been into a dark hole and emerged knows the truth of this, because when you emerge, you bring diamonds out of that darkness, and those diamonds can be of great service to others and to the whole. So the big question may look complex, but the answer is simple. Keep doing this inner work and out of that the perfect direction will emerge. Your dharma, your higher purpose, is the true direction in which you need to focus your energies.

So keep connecting inwardly and keep making bridges. Keep going with this work and then the outer world will begin to reflect to you what you are really here to do, and how you can be of the greatest service to the whole. Keep the faith, keep working, keep persevering and, in time, things will become easier for you. Even if, on the outer planes, all hell is breaking loose in the world, deep inside on the inner planes, deep clarity and peace will rule. In time, this will be conveyed to the outside world because it is on its way.

Amidst the ashes, a phoenix is rising, and it will bring a new world, a new Earth, a new kind of human, a new way of being, a paradigm shift, a quantum leap. This is what is coming, and many of us are anticipating it.

I bring this message of hope, but it is more than hope – for me it is certainty. It is for all of us, and if you go deep inside, you will feel it too. You will also feel a detachment about how it comes, because that is not in our hands. We each have a few lines of the script, and we can do our best to deliver our lines, but the plot is not ours. Yet it all unfolds with perfect timing, exactly as it is meant to.

THE AVATAR OF SYNTHESIS

I love the myths about the world saviour, and there are many versions. The Avatar of Synthesis is an ancient prophecy that is echoed in many great traditions, and can be found in the Book of Revelation, and in the Tibetan and Buddhist prophecies. This prophecy, taken from 'A Treatise on Cosmic Fire' by Alice A. Bailey, the theosophist, describes the coming of the great avatar, the Avatar of Synthesis who brings with them a massive transmutation:

'From the gates of gold down to the pit of earth, out from the flaming fire down to the circle of gloom, rideth the secret avatar, bearing the sword that pierceth. Naught can arrest His approach, and none may say Him nay. To the darkness of our sphere He rideth alone, and on His approach is seen the uttermost disaster, and the chaos of that which seeketh to withstand.

The fumes of utter blackness mount upwards in dissipation. The noise discordant of the warring elements greets the oncoming One and deters Him not. He passeth on His way, sweeping the circle of the spheres, and sounding forth the WORD.'

The avatar comes wielding a sword and riding on a white horse, and is a being of such vastness that it is said that it cannot incarnate in a single human body. It would blast that body into smithereens, instantly, as it would not be able to hold the frequency. So the higher initiates of the Christ Consciousness, the soul group that give themselves to the avatar, bow their heads and say, *'Come, inhabit us so that your presence may transform the lower planes, and knowingly we will be shattered in your bliss by your divine Shakti.'*

The soul group becomes the synarchy, and their sacrifice is represented by the horse, the sacrificial vessel.

There has always been a prophecy that the end will arrive in a great stage of surrender, making way for the great Oversoul. It is said that it can only come as far as the Mental Plane. It cannot come down to the Astral Plane or the Physical Plane as it is too powerful and would open the mind, shattering it, and stilling it instantly. But remnants of the Shakti would blast the lower planes, opening up the heart, transmuting the serpent energy of the astral plane, the *kundalini*, so that it is released from its cage of the body in a future age.

There are many revelations in the ancient scripts. In the Kalachakra Tantra, which is the greatest of the tantras from Tibet, you have the Kalki Rudra who brings the wheel of dharma, and wielding a flaming sword, speaks and puts an end to all chaos, and creates *samadhi* – a state of bliss and oneness – just through his words.

Of course, everyone wants to know when it will happen. But it has already begun. It comes at the end of the Kali Yuga, and it is beginning now, the end of the Dark Age, a time when humanity has completely forgotten its divine origins. It is a multi-generational explosion of Siddhis, which I call the 'Siddhic Supernova'. When it comes, and it will come, it will pick up pace as it opens and as the light returns.

THE DAWN OF THE BINARIES

Sometimes, when I re-read what I wrote about the 55th Gene Key, I feel shocked. Shocked that I wrote such prophetic, wild things, or perhaps they wrote themselves. One of the things mentioned is the Sacred Marriage, where two souls connect so deeply that they create the field of an enlightened consciousness by coming together. Part of the 55th Gene Key predicts that as it unlocks the higher frequencies in humanity, the phenomenon of the Sacred Marriage will occur more in the future, and it is one of the ways in which awakening will be unlocked. I feel deeply that this is true.

The 55th Gene Key is really about romance, in the true meaning of the word. What we see as romance in our films, our movies and our books is the beginning of understanding of what romance really is. But romance is life itself, the drama of the Maya, the illusion and the playing out of karma.

Part of the nature of this world is that it is all just a romantic dream. Towards the end of the dream, resolutions begin to occur more rapidly and as in any good romance, there is tension, a build up, then a shock, and a slow reunification, until the final ending of unity and redemption.

As the higher consciousness of the 55th Gene Key and the Freedom that comes with it start to enter humanity, and as our DNA starts to mutate, we are going to see more and more divine binary couples and relationships. This is where the consciousness of a human being, of a soul, or a Causal Body, divides into two, and then incarnates into two separate bodies for the purpose of finding each other, and awakening. It is one of the ways in which awakening is going to occur more and more in the future. And as the population naturally decreases, and the world starts to fall more silent, we will see the Binaries coming together and living in quiet places – in nature, I imagine – and with an extended life span, which is something else that will happen in the future.

The Binaries will be so self-contained that they will go through a process of absorption, where they become completely absorbed in each other's company. When you fall in love and you are immersed in the other person's aura, you become swallowed up by the love that unites you. Over time, that begins to fade for most people, but in the Binaries that love will not fade. It will go on coalescing, and it will go on purifying them. The depth of that love will purify the karma that lies in their ancestral lines to such a degree that they will become one enlightened consciousness in two bodies. Then their role may be complete, or on the other hand they may take on a new role and become, potentially, the true Mother-Father, and the linchpin of an awakening community.

A Binary couple may be two men or two women, and they may even be one human and one animal. That is also written into the future awakening. We have links and bridges to the animal and bird kingdoms, so we can form binary relationships with creatures as well. That is a specific kind of destiny, in which you share the same consciousness as the creature, whatever it is, you share the same consciousness, and it grows, and you learn from each other. It is beautiful, and a very specific karma, but it is still a binary relationship and so they will be locked into it. When one dies in the form, then the other one dies too. As in the purest form of romance, they die together or ascend together, absorbing as one into the Oversoul, and the bodies are just dropped.

In times to come, we will see all kinds of Binaries – deep loves coming into the world. It will be a very different world, a dream compared to the world that we have around us today. It won't be long coming. In just a few hundred years, the mutations will begin to drop into the human genome, and the Binaries will begin to drop in among us and will spread, and there will be more and more of them. Love will begin to burgeon, and links and bridges will connect all the realms, the dream realms, between the male, the female, the human and the animal, because every creature and every thing has a correspondence with our genome, through the Siddhis.

So when the 37th Siddhi of Tenderness unlocks, it resonates with every dog, just as the 40th Siddhi of Divine Will has a resonance with every cat. If a Siddhi unlocks somewhere in your genome, there is the potential to reach across the divide and connect in some way with one or all of the corresponding creatures. These are the Gene Keys teachings of the Dream Arc – profound teachings that connect humanity in a much deeper way to nature and the creatures surrounding us.

The Binaries are coming and they will bring a new kind of romance that will dawn in our world. Our romantic dreams will be realised, and just as our romantic films and stories end in that sweet, tender way, it will be the same for us, in our incarnation cycles. If it is in our destiny, in our dharma, then that will be the way in which we awaken. The finale of many people's cycles of incarnation will end with the Binaries.

A very different world is coming. We cannot imagine it. Well, we can, but we will need a big imagination.

JETSUN DOLMA
TRANSFORMATION THROUGH THE FEMININE

Sometimes I have visitations in my inner life, and one such visitation was from a female being who had been haunting my dreams and meditations for a while. I did not know who it was at the time, but when she left me her name, it kept going around in my head... Jetsun Dolma... Jetsun Dolma. I had to look it up. I knew it had the ring of a Tibetan name, and it turned out that Jetsun Dolma is the great female Buddha, who is also known as Tara in Tibetan Culture.

Tara comes in different forms in a range of colours that symbolise different aspects of her. Her colours are White Tara – Black Tara – Red Tara – Yellow Tara – Green Tara – Blue Tara, and sometimes she is represented with her different Tara forms surrounding her in a rainbow. They are all emanations of her Bodhisattvic enlightened energy, and have different purposes and roles in the world. What it opens up for me is that this is the stream that is moving humanity into its next phase, into the next epoch, the stream of the Divine Feminine.

What is the Divine Feminine? People talk about it, but what does it mean? Certainly, it is to do with women, but it is also to do with men. The Divine Feminine is inside each of us, inside everything, and imbued in every level within creation. It has a very specific role of transforming the consciousness of the world as a whole and so it is something to really consider moving forwards, moving into a new chapter of our evolution, because it is the Divine Feminine that will be doing the actual activity. It is the Ray of Active Intelligence that will actually create a new world. And this will happen because it is the mother energy. Although the yang has its role, the only way you can transform a whole species is through the mother.

The iconic representations are that Yin is water and Yang is fire. The Yin has watery qualities like gentleness, patience, wisdom and intuition, and is more mysterious, whereas the Yang has qualities of action, passion and reason. We have created a world based upon the Yang, although there have been flashes of Yin when feminine intuition has led to great inventions that have helped us to move forward. But, essentially, we have created a world based upon logic and reason, which has improved the world on many levels, particularly the external, but on the internal not so much.

The questions of the internal, of the Yin, are, *'How do you feel inside yourself? How is your inner world, the shape of your inner world? Are you fulfilled? Are you happy? Are you authentic?'* Until our species asks these questions as seriously as any other question, we cannot create the world we all dream of, a peaceful world where humans are in harmony with each other and their environment.

The Yin, the feminine, the Tara, brings this transition, and it will take place through women, empowered women. An empowered woman is something wonderful to behold, although perhaps she is not what many of us might think, and she is not a woman trying to behave like a man. In the feminine qualities of the Yin, her strength is in her patience, gentleness and yielding, and in her intuition, which cuts through all the logic and mind stuff, and goes straight to the core.

Women are going to rebuild our world on many levels and none more so than mothers, because the mother can shape the child in the womb. When the mother pours her love and her quality of care into that foetus, she sculpts that little boy or little girl, and she creates a creature of integrity and beauty.

That is one way in which the world can be transformed. Another is through a much more powerful focus on the Yin, on the feminine qualities. You might think that those qualities are weak in comparison to the big showy energy of the Yang, the egoic fire that gets things done – but does it? Actually, it often gets things done but they may be the wrong things, so they cause more chaos.

The Yin is the power of softness, the power of waiting, the power of clarity that comes through time. Think about this whether you are a woman or a man. If you feel you have been wronged by someone, burn them with the power of your forgiveness, that is your revenge. Do not go after them, let them go and love them. The only way you can be free of someone who has wronged you in some way is to love them and forgive them. When you forgive them, you burn them with their own shame, and that is not in a negative way. You let them feel the quality of their shame, because they need to face up to what they have done, and the only way they are going to do that is by feeling your forgiveness. That is an example of empowered femininity and it can be in a man or a woman. It is not about gender – don't get confused by gender, that is just the equipment. We are talking about the essence.

So, consider these things as we move forward into this epoch of the empowered feminine, within the male and within the female. For the male, our job is to empower through our support, our love, our care, and through being available, yet vulnerable and strong at the same time, through being a whole man. That will allow these empowered women all over the world to begin to reshape our civilisation. Their voices are being heard more and more and, as they are heard, balance will return to our societies and our civilisations. I think this will be an extremely beautiful and powerful time.

Jetsun Dolma, we welcome you.

THE DALLIANCE

Every word has a teaching. The word 'dalliance' came to me one day on my morning walk with my dogs, by a beautiful river in Devon, the river Dart, where I often see dragonflies, damselflies, kingfishers and other magical creatures. That morning I saw a pair of kingfishers, beautiful little birds adorned in iridescent blue, gold and orange. They were in a dalliance, dancing, and they came together for a flashing moment of bejewelled splendour, shrieking in wild, piping jubilation. Perhaps they were also territorial sounds, or maybe it was a male and a female, but they kept clashing together like two bursts of rainbows. It was exquisite. It was a moment of ecstasy, and it went off in the atrium of my heart, and then the word came out, the *dalliance* of the kingfishers.

Walt Whitman wrote a lovely, short poem called 'The Dalliance of the Eagles', and there are many other creatures which can be seen in dalliance. If you are ever near a river and you see dragonflies, or damselflies, you will often see them in dalliances where they come and land on each other and then chase one another. It is the dalliance of the dragonflies.

Watching those kingfishers got me contemplating, looking at life from deep time, which is something I am increasingly doing as I explore the art of contemplation. One of the things that is central to contemplation is beginning to look at life from deep time. Contemplating deep time means spanning out, far beyond your lifetime, and examining some of the ways in which evolution moves across decades, centuries and millennia, then entire epochs, and what the ancients called *yugas*, which are huge cycles of time. And moving beyond that into the life and death of a universe, and other universes that spawned this universe, and even vaster cycles, that are infinite and eternal.

Reflecting on deep time is a way of playing within the field of time, and the illusion of time, in a way, but also playing with it in a more broad way, and to realise that wherever we are submerged in time, whatever scale you look at, what you are seeing is a dalliance. You are seeing two forces coming together in a brief flash, then parting and coming together again. They come together in a flash of play and brilliance and music and revelry, and sometimes sacrifice and surrender.

Dalliance is a word that we also use when someone has had an affair, or a short relationship. *'We had a dalliance,'* it was over as soon as it had begun but it was joyful while it lasted. Our whole lives are made of dalliances. A 50-year-long marriage is a dalliance, till death comes and parts you, and you go back into the whole. Then you come back out and you have another dalliance. You will have many dalliances in your life that are fleeting and ephemeral, beautiful and magnificent. And they are here to be indulged in, to be played in, to be celebrated. That is what the word is suggesting, that the spirit of play is alive in this word dalliance. And it is a spirit that we need more and more as times seem to get heavier, and we move into a time of great transition for this planet, for our species and all other species.

The dalliances of species that are becoming extinct will come to an end. But new species will be born, or maybe return in another form, in another universe, Nothing is lost, ever, when you look at life from deep time, because the cosmos consists of universal fractal patterns, like universal soundbites or data bytes of universal information, which are never lost. They cannot be lost because they exist at every level in the cosmos.

We live in a holographic universe in which these codes are constantly reforming and reshaping themselves in endless possibilities, endless, infinite dalliances. As one force meets another force, they transform each other, and something new is born from it. Then they go back to the formless, and then again another and another, over and over again, male, female, yin, yang. And the offspring that are born from those dalliances, from those opposite poles, will go on to create further dalliances and possibilities.

It is useful to look at life through the lens of a word like dalliance, particularly in difficult times, and to see it as a whole, to see it as an epoch that we are moving into, a change of season for our species and for our planet. And a new dalliance will emerge as the old one fades, as those two kingfishers drift off in their different directions. Who knows where they go? But then they come together again and again, the cosmic cymbals clashing together. And we need this spirit inside us to face what is coming. Are we going to face it with tight, closed minds and hearts, and with fear? Because if we face the future from that place, we are going to create something that is much worse. We need to face it with a sense of perspective, so that we can face it with creativity, and sometimes with rebelliousness.

Dalliance is the energy of vitality. It is rebellious and wants to challenge. There can be sword-clashing sometimes in dalliance. But there is also a playfulness, even within the seriousness of life and with all the suffering in the world.

I often think of the refugees I saw at the Idomeni refugee camp in Greece, people who had lost their homes, and were living in poverty, with nothing, in a tent by a road, and there were more and more arriving. I was so moved and shocked to see it all. Yet, here we are, clicking on 'add to basket' and 'buy now'. It is all so easy for privileged people like us.

Even to be discussing dalliance and lightness when there is all that suffering, how do we hold that paradox? And yet we have to have that serious play, that playful seriousness, so that we can face the future in the spirit of creativity. To be able to meet it through our hearts, because it is the heart and the compassion of the heart that the world needs, not more misery, not more reaction, not more anger. Any anger should not be expressed through blame and complaint, but transformed into passion.

We need to face the future in this spirit of dalliance, because at some point in the future this whole phase will be over. It will be gone and something else will be in its place. Even if the Earth isn't here, something else will be. A fresh dalliance of life force will be occurring somewhere else. It always will.

We are eternal beings, eternally caught in these dramas and beautiful plays and dalliances with each other. As we move forward we need a fresh view of life that reflects this and comes from the heart. Open heart, open mind. Soft heart, soft, yielding mind – at times.

So, whatever life brings you, enjoy your dalliance today, and each day to come.

PACKING AWAY THE WORLD

When my father passed away, I spent a lot of time dealing with his estate and packing away his things. It was a very long process. I had been in the privileged position of growing up in a house with my parents and my brother and sister in the house where we were born and lived our whole childhoods, never living anywhere else. After my mother died, my father stayed and he went on living there till he died at the age of ninety-four.

I had a powerful stability in my life from this one house that I could always go back to. It was a beautiful house with a big garden, set among trees and woods. I have many memories of it, and packing away the house was a bit like packing away my childhood. Having gone through the process of packing it all away and letting go, I left the house for the last time, knowing I would never go there again. Then I experienced a huge revelation, that I was living inside a metaphor, a metaphor for humanity right now, for our planet. That metaphor grew deeper and richer for me, and the prophecy that I bring as a possibility for you to consider is that we, our generation and the next few generations, are packing away the world right now.

It is a similar process to the one that my brother and sister and I went through as we packed away a lifetime of things and memories, objects and old ways. The house that my parents and we three children all lived in was never changed or updated. The wiring and the plumbing were really old and probably dangerous, and I imagined that the new owners would gut the whole house and start again. Whatever they decided, they would bring their own vision.

It is like that with us. We still have the old paradigms and the old ways of doing things, but there is a new wave coming that will clean out the world in some way. So it can be an unsettling time, but also an exciting time to be growing something new within the same house.

We are packing away an old way of being, new occupants are arriving, a new generation is coming in, and there will be a period when the house lies empty. This is when the cleaners come to deep clean everything. Then the new arrivals will bring their vision and their dream, and it will be nothing to do with you. You have to let go, and you will not know what is coming. What if you were to view life like this right now? You might live in a different way, in a lighter way.

When you are packing something away, there are things that you do. You might want to say blessings and give thanks, or perhaps you have a feast to celebrate how things have been, and then you let things go with grace and with gratitude. This might be a way of looking at your life right now. It doesn't mean you don't get on with your life, but if there is an energy coming in to sweep the world clean, and if we are going to empty out the world in some way so that a new force, a new energy, a new paradigm, a new human can come in, then it will change the way we look at life today.

Humans tend to believe that things are going to keep going in the same direction, for example, assuming that we are going to get to Mars, or that we are going to evolve new technologies that will save us. We may take for granted that will be the way of things. But I don't believe it is the case. The implications are huge, and it means that you won't want to consume so much as it is unsustainable to continue growing and expanding as we are. We have to cut down on and simplify everything and live more lightly, with fewer of us.

Of course there are a lot of concerns: we worry about the environment and all the creatures that we share the earth with, but perhaps they are also part of this. Perhaps everything has to be minimised, but remember that nothing is ever lost. The DNA of all beings continues. It continues because the amino acid structures out of which life was built are the same for all of us, for all life on this planet. So new life can always be built, it is just a matter of time. It could be another 100,000 years before what was extinct can be rebuilt, but these periods have come and gone before for species on this planet.

So I find 'packing away the world' a powerful metaphor. How will we pack it away with grace? It doesn't mean we should not make a stand and be fierce warriors of justice. That is part of our finale, to make a stand, to really stand for that which we love, and all of the causes that move us. But knowing that this is coming, this huge change, this great change, your expectations of yourself might lessen a little, and your judgements of others might also soften. You might find a new compassion growing inside you, and a lighter touch, so that you can let things go and also embrace a beautiful potential future.

Another layer to this metaphor is that if you feel sad at the thought of not being here to enjoy that new future, that paradigm, then remember there is always sadness in times of transition. Yet if you know that you are an immortal soul and that there is a continuity of consciousness, then the soul that is inside you is the guest that will come in the future – it is you, it is us.

We will return in different forms and in a different consciousness. Which is not just a fantasy but a great cause for celebration. If you have that quiet knowing inside yourself, then a good use of this time is to strengthen those inner connections to the continuity of consciousness and to your soul, which has lived through so many lifetimes and, in the deep past that is outside time and space, has been through transitions perhaps even greater than this one. This great metaphor, this great allegory that we are living in is an extraordinary time.

So how will you pack away your world? How will you live differently, in a lighter way? These are the questions. There may not be some magical thing that saves us all. It may be that this is how it has to be. There has to be a closing down, a wiping the slate clean, and the Earth in its awesome resilience will reboot in a new form over generations. And that means that the generations that are here during the transition are extraordinary.

Consider when there is a big weather system on the horizon. If you live by the ocean, and a massive storm arrives that sweeps everything before it, everyone goes indoors. Most people hunker down, in their bolt-holes, and yet certain people come out: big wave surfers, people who specialise in riding storms. When we look at children coming into the world now, perhaps that is who they are, big wave surfers, specialised beings who come in specifically at times of massive change to ride the change, because they want the exhilaration, the risk of that metamorphosis. Every generation is equipped, internally, specifically for its time. So we need not worry about that as parents, as an older generation passing over.

There are things at work in the world that we don't always understand. Yet, here am I, a prophet, and prophets are always outside their time and space, and often laughed at or doubted and sometimes considered crazy. Only time will tell whether what I am saying is true.

This is only something to think about – how you might live in a different way if it were true, and open your heart and mind even more. Then you might start to live in the way that specifically the Earth needs you to live. It need not dampen your enthusiasm, your passion or your zeal for justice and truth and for things to be right, and to challenge things that are done in the old way. But it will give you a new way of seeing things. It will light the flame of hope in your heart. It will give you a sense of deep purpose and also a tinge of sadness, but also a great joy for what is to come, and a sense of continuity.

I hope that this idea actually gives you more purpose and a greater perspective, and builds links within that will enable you to surf this change and to see it as a beautiful, positive thing. Even though many may suffer, the population may decrease significantly, our cupboards may empty out, we may pack things away, and there may be fewer and fewer of us here. There may be suffering, great suffering, potentially, but it is all part of the letting-go.

So we must stay close to each other and build our bonds together, and connect back to the Earth. We have to live more simply and more lightly at this time, and lessen our expectations of what might happen. We might be able to save the Earth, but we may not be able to save it in the way that our minds currently conceive.

There are new guests coming, and we do not know how things will change. But as the tempest comes and flushes out the old, we can greet it with openness, understanding and clarity.

I encourage you to open your heart, open your mind and soften into this time of packing away the world...

If you consider this metaphor deeply, you will see where it resonates inside you. If it doesn't resonate, throw it out. Forget all about this, and me, and move on your own trajectory into the future, into the now.

Fragments of Light
Chapter 5

A RELAXING TRUTH

The idea that we are reborn again and again, with the chance of repeating our lessons here on Earth, and that we incarnate with our loved ones in soul groups to live our lives together over and over can be really comforting and reassuring.

Although many of us feel drawn to exploring our past lives, and there is much that can be learned from our previous incarnations and relationships, what is most exciting is setting the trajectory for our future self, laying the foundation and igniting the spark for the creation of that future being.

IS IT REAL?
REINCARNATION AND REBIRTH — PART 1

Is there such a thing as reincarnation? What is it? Many spiritual teachers and teachers of wisdom are asked this, and of course there are many opinions.

When Christ said, *'In my Father's house are many mansions,'* I think he was saying that there are many layers of reality that we can exist in. There are gradations of frequency, and all realities, excepting the ultimate reality, are relative. They have a relativity to them, a relative truth. The ultimate truth is beyond words and concepts.

You might say, *'What's the point in adopting a relative truth?'* The answer is that relative truths are like the rungs on a ladder that lead to the absolute truth. So if a relative truth gives you an improved life and puts you at ease, why would you not adopt it? That is a great question to begin with.

You can look at different truths as you would books on a shelf. You pick out a truth, and if it resonates with you, you take it as your truth and decide to live by it. We all pull out these books, these concepts, from the shelves of existence and then we live by them. Sometimes we discard them and open a new one, have some kind of a breakthrough, or even a breakdown, and then we take a different book, a different truth. That is life as a human, and it is how the mind operates. So, reincarnation is one of those mansions, one of those layers, and one of those levels.

There is a lovely quote from 1928 by Henry Ford, the American industrialist – the car man – he was a big fan of reincarnation:

'I adopted the theory of reincarnation when I was twenty-six. Religion offered nothing to the point. Even work could not give me complete satisfaction. Work is futile if we cannot utilise the experience we collect in one life in the next. When I discovered reincarnation, it was as if I had found a universal plan. I realised that there was a chance to work out my ideas. Time was no longer limited, I was no longer a slave to the hands of the clock.

Genius is experience. Some seem to think that it is a gift or talent, but it is the fruit of long experience in many lives. The discovery of reincarnation put my mind at ease. If you preserve a record of this conversation, write it so that it puts men's minds at ease. I would like to communicate to others the calmness that the long view of life gives to us.'

This view has been central to the Hindu culture for thousands of years, and has its advantages and disadvantages. Some say it will make us lazy, *'Oh well I will have another life.'* Personally, at the level my mind operates within these layers, I find it a very relaxing truth, as Henry Ford did.

Within the fabric of the cosmos, rebirth is something we see everywhere, and there is a great deal of evidence out there that points to reincarnation. For instance, there have been many children found to have clear memories of their previous lives, and there are records of this that you can find online, and a lot to be found on the subject. However, I am not interested in proving it; I just want to show the validity of a healthy viewpoint. As long as you understand it as that, it has a relative truth. Then you can adopt it and make use of it, and it may lead you somewhere, as it did for Henry Ford. He discovered that it enabled him to relax and take a much longer view. I am a bit like that too with the work I do, as I am really interested in the bigger picture of helping this planet.

There is another view that we have been conditioned with, a kind of pressure, that comes from the non-dualists (for example, the Buddhists, who I love), which is that we take no views at all, or else all views are false, which is true. But then there is the pressure on those who believe that, *'We've got to become enlightened – we've got to get it all done.'* That pressure can sometimes create a tension in us, a kind of pressured spiritual conditioning which could create a good or a bad tension, *'I've got to get enlightened. I can't hold any views as they are all false.'* This can put you in a kind of funk. But if that is your path, then that is your path, you should celebrate it and go for it – but then this may not be of so much interest to you.

One of the great vows that has come out of Buddhism is the Boddhisattva vow, which is the vow that a soul takes to never leave this plane until all are enlightened. In other words, to keep coming back and be reborn into the world and help bring everyone out of the Maya and towards the light. It is a wonderful vow and it leads to a deeply compassionate view of the world. If you have some work that you want to achieve on the human plane, the long-term view is very generous. If you see it as multi-generational work, then it could be something you perceive yourself as incarnating back into to continue.

The work of the Gene Keys that I am doing is creating a synthesis of world teachings and a global community who are able to come into the embodiment of the teachings together, over time – and it does take time. Even with having the resources to be able to manifest things on the physical plane, it takes a long time. Also, people are dying and new people are being born, and so there is a whole story unfolding all the time. If you place yourself in the wider context of that, you can really see where you want to be going.

Often, we focus on our past lives and who we were, and the karma we brought with us into this life. But I am more interested in who I am going to be, because who I am going to be is being created and imprinted out of how I am now, from my thoughts and my behaviour. So I am setting my trajectory into the future, which can be a really beautiful thing.

There is also a part of us that wants to get out of this game, because we suffer here and sometimes it's really not fun! But I think that is a stage that we have to get past, until we really enjoy being here. Why not linger, why not do some work here? Why not see it as, *'I have a project, a global project, potentially, that I want to be part of with others, with the community, with a family of people I love, who I want to meet again. I want to come back into this, carry on this work and go deeper and refine my spiritual path.'* So give yourself that gift. With this view, you can set your future trajectory from the present.

Going back into the past may have its uses, although it has been said that if you were to remember all your lives, your brain would not be able to handle it and you would go mad, because there are so many lives and so many layers to each life. You have been around for so long, and you have experienced every conceivable aspect of planetary behaviour, crisis, conflict, suffering, love, sex, joy, all of it. It is all part of who you are. It has led you here and to a spiritual path of awakening, where you can begin to draw on all that experience that your soul has. There is an aspect of your soul that retains that wisdom, that enables you to see further, to have clarity, love more, and accelerate your own evolution.

In one of the deep mystical experiences I had in the past, I saw the algorithms of incarnation. I saw that everything has mathematics and a formula and an algorithm. If you knew these algorithms, you would see the path of all your lives, and the strand that connects you to them through space-time while you are here on this planet, living out your lessons on this evolutionary journey. You can even project it into the future because it is connected to timelines and dates, and you can work everything out. When I came out of that state, I did not retain the memory of all the algorithms and the details, and I had an insight that was, *'Well what would be the point? Isn't it more important to live inside this theatre, this current world stage, and fully inhabit these bodies that we are in?'*

One day I will probably explore the possibilities of incarnative cycles. Having this broader view and really adopting it releases a lot of fear and tension, particularly around death and dying. It means that we can die consciously, and seed the trajectory of where we want to go. And when we are ready to leave, we will leave everything behind and ascend to another plane. Wonderful.

So we can allow ourselves the thought that, *'Well, maybe I will come back. That might be nice, and I will get to see my loved ones in other forms. It may be that I won't remember them on a mental level, but I will remember them on a cellular level, in the cells of my being.'*

Reincarnation is a fascinating realm with many things to think about, digest and contemplate, and many different strands woven into it. It can be really healthy to adopt it, but it is a subject you can be playful with, so hold it lightly.

'In my Father's house are many mansions.' Which ones will you inhabit?

THE PERMANENT ATOM
REINCARNATION AND REBIRTH – PART 2

Traditional psychology essentially blames our life and our personality on our heredity and our environment, which allows you to shift blame away from yourself in some subtle way. Whereas the teachings about karma, which come from Buddhism and other ancient religions, say that you cannot transfer blame outside yourself for anything, and it is all on you. That does not mean that it is your fault, but it means that it is for you and by you and, more than that, you have before you the perfect ingredients for the next phase of your growth, your evolution. That is really the essence of what karma is about, and it is rooted, perhaps, in the ancient tradition of initiation, which is based on the idea that we are evolving spiritually, not just physically.

As we evolve through a world and a universe made of frequencies, every now and again we transcend the level that we are on and move to a higher frequency. That paradigm shift is called an initiation, and sometimes they are sudden, and sometimes very slow. The ancient mystery schools would perform their initiations in secret, but now the secret of initiation is an open secret, as the real initiations take place in everyday life, as, in fact, they always have.

When we are looking at the idea of reincarnation, or rebirth (as I prefer to say), we have to look at the soul. I call this the Causal Body, a subtle, higher-dimensional body which is part of who we are and is the part that survives death. Some teachings call it the 'permanent atom', almost as if there is one atom inside us that survives death over and over. In a sense, that is the Causal Body: a subtle essence that maintains a kind of evolutionary story as it incarnates and reincarnates.

Over aeons, you get to polish this body, this atom, and each lifetime can be devoted to polishing a single virtue. Think of your life now. Perhaps there is one single virtue that you are here to polish. It could be forgiveness or sacrifice or self-love, or perhaps it is self-forgiveness, which seems to be a pretty universal one. It might be developing extraordinary art or music, or some other great form of service that you are here to perfect in this life. Or it could be finding ways of tackling the trauma that life brings us.

What happens through this notion of incarnation is that we take on a wound, a core wound, and we take it on for the sake of the whole. We come here to repair and transform that wound, some broken part of the world, and we are an aspect of that wound. The Kabbalists call this the Tikkun Olam. It is about allowing our suffering to cut us so deeply that it cleans us and awakens us, and we are here then to transcend the suffering. Think of the intense grief that some of us have to go through. It might be the loss of a loved one, even the loss of a child. The intensity of those levels of grief can propel us to a higher initiation, to a higher level of consciousness where we become aware of the transcendent.

I was amazed when I read that in the UK, where we are generally a rather conservative and reserved group of people, one in three people believe in angels. *'Is this really true?'* I thought to myself, *'They're keeping very quiet about it!'* It was very revealing, that even in this modern, materialistic, science-based culture that we live in, which is all based on looking for external fulfilment, there is a deep feeling in us that there may be something more, and people want to believe in angels. Science and materialism can do great damage, even for all the wonderful things they bring us, because they can really damage subtler worldviews, like the perfection of the notion of reincarnation, and angels.

There is a saying, a 'ring-pass-not', which means that, as a whole, we don't remember our previous lives, because we forget them as we come through into form. When we go out, we remember them again, but when we come back through the veil they are once again forgotten. Could you invent a more perfect and beautiful game? Your awareness grows as you transcend the thoughts, opinions and worldviews you have taken on, and as you access those more ancient memories, even though they are not specific, but more general memories, the Causal Body becomes more resplendent and more shining.

In every life we are given a task to fulfil, a higher purpose. How do we find what it is? We find it through realising that every event in our life is pointing us directly at that higher purpose, and especially the suffering, which is not just suffering for the sake of suffering, but pointing you towards a higher purpose. In the alchemy of rebirth, we have lives of suffering, and you might say that some of us are 'doing time' for dark deeds that we have done in the past. There might be some truth in that, because that is how karma operates. But there is also the possibility if you are a more advanced soul, or perhaps have more shine and radiance because you have done more work on yourself, that you might choose to take on more suffering. How might you tell those two apart? It is how they deal with the suffering.

There are those that cave in and just give way, blaming others and becoming lost and hopeless. Then there are those who rise through it. This may be explained by individual karma and collective karma. Once you have purified the individual karma, you take on the collective karma, the karma of the whole, because you have burnt up all your own from the past memories of things that you did.

Collective karma has a different quality. It feels more weighty, but it also feels less connected to you. All human beings are actually sharing in the karma of the whole, and all deeds belong to all of us. Then the higher souls may come in and may take on more karma for the sake of the whole, and this is the Christ impulse, the realisation of the Christ.

Once the soul has passed all the exams here in 'Earth School', it will leave the university and enter the universal, the eternal, and that consciousness is then permanently aware of itself as eternal. It can move onto higher spheres and higher levels of union and wholeness, until it merges with the entirety, the Divine. Earth is the ultimate classroom.

We think that time and space are real, as we are governed by them, and yet in our Causal Body we have a memory of eternity. Consciousness incarnates from pure eternal awareness down into the deep material realms and forgets itself so that it can remember itself. It dives into the illusion of time and space, the Maya. If consciousness did not do this there would be no story. If there were no time and no space, there would be no story. The purpose of this higher human perception is to pierce the storylines of incarnation and rise up through them.

You might ask, 'What is the point in this?' But we can't really ask why, although, of course, 'Why?' is the quintessential human question. In this case only our ascension and transcendence can answer why. We may find that there is no answer, and it just is. But 'it just is' does not satisfy the human mind, only the divine mind, which can accept simply the will and the mystery of the whole.

So consider your life from this perspective of rebirth. What are you dealing with right now? How are you dealing with it? What marks are you getting in your exams? There is always room for improvement, and of course you can sit the same exam again and again. Are you going to come back? Why not excel in your exams? Why not assume everything is your responsibility? Everything is for you.

Every drama is created by your higher self so that you can transform it and transcend it. That is the central message of my teachings of the Gene Keys. *Every Shadow contains a Gift.* How many diamonds can you find in the darkness of your life, in the coalface of your suffering? Once you start finding them, you can begin working for the wider whole and help others find their diamonds. Then we can live lives of deep service, wishing only to serve the whole and transform the darkness around us.

We ask the great compassionate question, '*What is the highest service I can offer the whole during this life, during this incarnation?*' And then we live that question.

RECIPROCAL LUMINOSITY
REINCARNATION AND REBIRTH – PART 3

One of the greatest sufferings of humanity is the grief that we go through when we lose those we love, whether when we are the one dying or the one staying behind. Surely the worst kind of grief is one that has no belief and no faith, and holds the idea of just a dropping away into nothingness. It may not be your viewpoint, but it is the materialistic viewpoint of our current age. But what if we did not have to feel that desperate grief of love and loss? What if we knew that we could never be separated from those whom we love? What if our loved ones were like the waves of the ocean?

If we were to bring our focus off the individual wave and, instead, bring our awareness into the ocean, then we would never need to suffer that kind of loss. It would be rather like saying farewell to the guests at a party, knowing that we will see them again soon.

There is a great notion that we incarnate in soul groups, in fractals, collectivities or constellations, like crystals – permanent atoms that can interlock perfectly to form geometric symmetries of consciousness. Such consciousness surrounds our planet like a luminous shroud. Souls, or shards of consciousness, are individuating and undulating wave patterns dancing through time and space. The whole pattern is constantly evolving. So your mother in one life is your child in another life and your brother in another, and your enemy in another, but always connecting with you, always playing out a theatre of evolution. We travel together in these symmetries, across continents, across gene pools, across eons of time. Then there is awakening and when awakening comes, it moves like a virus down the lineages, radiating outwards.

So all our relationships, whether they are good, bad, happy or sad, become a repository of awakening as we trigger more light and growth in each other. The more challenging a relationship is, the greater its potential to trigger our inner luminosity, what I call 'reciprocal luminosity', and we share the light with each other, through our relationships.

We play out the shadow patterns, and then, when we are ready, we play out the transformation of those shadows through forgiveness, tolerance, compassion and kindness, through all the dramas that take place in the relationships in all of our lives.

What of the enduring myth of the twin soul, the perfect lover, the binary flame that perfectly matches our own? This is a myth we find woven into the drama of the reincarnating soul. We sense a truth in it and covet it through our art, our music, romance and dramas. We long for a perfect union with another. It has been said that we get to be with our twin soul twelve times only in all our incarnations, twelve times in twelve eons. It is a myth – but who knows?

We dream of a life where we rest with our beloved, the crystal that interlocks perfectly with our own, the *Vesica Piscis*, the myth of perfect, true love, and this memory lives in us in each lifetime. It may be that we meet this twin soul many times, but we cannot be with them because they end up married to another or perhaps the timing is just off. Perhaps they incarnated as our brother, our mother or even our child. Perhaps the wounds we carry in this particular life are just too great to make it possible for us to be together, or perhaps we incarnate as enemies and we destroy each other, or perhaps one stays out of the form while the other is in, and all we feel is a deep, lonely ache of the loss because we cannot feel them here.

The drama is Shakespearean. It is unendingly beautiful in its ache, but it is here simply to teach us, so that we can learn to open, to grow, forgive and let go, and one day begin to transcend the drama itself, even the drama of perfect love. This is the purpose of it all, to slowly learn to become detached, the Great teachers have guided us towards this, to let go of the outer quest for love and for truth, which is always ephemeral, and to seek the eternal within. We have to come to this Great Truth. As our awareness of it grows, our love grows with it and truth is revealed within us like a memory, and so we begin to awaken. We see that we are playing a role, and a detachment arises as we surrender deeper into the whole, into the drama and the dance.

With this detachment comes a vast love, a love that transcends any individual connections. So when a loved one dies, we remember that they live inside our heart and our heart is eternal. They are actually a part of our greater collective body. Each soul group, each constellation, interlocks with another and another, to form the great collectivity of humanity's higher self, the Oversoul, a higher collective beyond our comprehension.

Reciprocal luminosity is like a supernova. It triggers greater and greater awakening and inner light, and there is only one direction on the path. While good and evil are played out on the stage, the awakening of truth is beyond both, although as Swami Vivekananda said, 'Good is very close to truth.' And so the story goes on. Incarnations come and go, and we polish the jewel of our being as we draw light from all those around us. When one awakens, grace pours through that whole lineage, that fractal, and within a few generations the whole fractal awakens in a chain reaction, like the petals of a flower. This is the dance and the drama to contemplate.

Consider also the image of the sun, because the sun is our planet in the future. You probably think of the sun as a turbulent mass of hydrogen and helium, as our scientists say. And it is that, but what if it is more? If you deconstruct a human body, all you find is the elements. You will never find the indwelling soul. How would anyone find that? I came across an article by a scientist who was trying to prove that life after death cannot exist because we know how atoms behave. It seemed like a desperate materialistic mind clinging to the wreckage of a sinking ship.

In my view, the sun is an earth that has already ascended, and all the chains of its being, all the families of its individuated awareness, all the collectivities, constellations and soul groups have realised their collective oversoul. The luminosity triggered a chain reaction at the core and the result is a collective awakening far beyond our understanding. That is where we are heading. It first began millennia ago, but the chain reaction is starting now, in this current epoch, as more and more individuals are waking up through the drama and realising their divinity.

So it begins, the beginning of the end of reincarnation itself. For, when the whole begins to realise what it is through its parts, the game is over.

For me, the very presence of the sun is evidence of the eternal, even though we know that the sun too will one day die. It is a symbol of the inner truth, and the outer is modelled on the inner. The earth revolves, night comes, and every morning we are born again. The sun remains constant, and it is we who move. It shines even in the depths of night, and it is the same with us, as even in the depths of our suffering, our eternal flame is burning as brightly as ever.

Contemplate these things, particularly when you are next around those who are dying. Remind yourself that you will not be apart from this being who is leaving. It is a temporary farewell, a veil drawn over your eyes but never drawn over your heart. Our heart knows the truth of eternity. All our beloveds live forever inside our heart, and they are part of the one heart.

Let death awaken an even greater love inside you. And let the passing of a loved one be the wave that carries you into the great ocean where all hearts are one heart.

GLOBAL TRANSFORMATION
REINCARNATION AND REBIRTH – PART 4

In part one, I mentioned the mystical experience where I saw the algorithms of incarnation. I saw that the whole of humanity is one collective consciousness, one organism, and everything is permeated by a perfect sort of preconceived pulsing which has a mathematical basis to it.

The consciousness of the whole, the Divine, has come down into this human experience, and then split up into shards, fractals and mathematical geometries. It goes through an amazing, pulsing breath pattern as it forgets itself and then comes into form over and over again, down the beautiful, infinite fractal lines. Each line has to get back to its source, like the serpent consuming its own tail, like the *ouroboros* of the Greek mystery. That is our journey as a species, as it is our journey as an individual, and there is a perfection to the unravelling.

It can be helpful to think that there is a pattern in the unfolding of that evolutionary story, that arc, and within the layers of the story there are grand epochs of consciousness diving into the form, forgetting themselves while remembering themselves. We are in an epoch now, and an epoch may be thousands or millions of years. The epochs are separated by major events, often cataclysmic ones, because as each epoch shifts and as the journey shifts, the whole consciousness of humanity starts to remember more of itself. There is a kind of birth canal that we have to move through as a species, as the species itself mutates.

It is a great journey, and behind it is the notion that there are whole epochs that have occurred in the past, that are no longer accessible to us, beyond recorded history. All we can do is look back as far as we can and we come to Neanderthals, cave men, Cro-Magnon and the early prehistoric primates, and so on. But beyond all that evolutionary history that we can follow are other histories, other chains or rounds of civilisation when we were a completely different being, and before that there was another epoch, also forgotten.

Each epoch is separated by a big birth-death event, and so the memories of previous epochs are not consciously held in the storylines of humans, although they are there as imprints in our myths. We remember them unconsciously and, interestingly, they are also remembered by the plant realm, the insects and the creatures who hold the memory, but particularly the plants. Some plant medicines can release the floodgates between the cataclysms and open up the memories. They can take you way back and way forward, because in the timeless realm, out of form, all is known and all is seen, while here in the form we are deeply embedded in time and space, story and drama.

We are now on the cusp of a new epoch. This is the deep insight that I stand behind and which underpins the Gene Keys as a set of teachings. Before the epoch changes, a lot of things change rapidly. A lot of memories come back and a lot of awakening begins to occur as a ripple passes through the whole and begins to shake the system, the whole constellation, the entire web. The whole thing begins to quiver and then, we enter periods of crisis and there is a shakedown. A tornado is coming as things begin to fall apart at a global level and there are signs that a cataclysmic shift may be coming.

Human beings have thought that there was going to be a cataclysm coming for millennia, but that is not what I am referring to. It is more that a big shift is coming with the epoch change and we cannot envisage what lies ahead. We cannot envisage the next mutation of human beings. It is not really possible for us, within this bio-vehicle, to fully understand the next one, because the next one will be a paradigm shift, a quantum leap.

In this cycle of incarnation, the whole species moves through a portal, and the veil that separates us between one dimension and the next begins to dissolve. This happens particularly as we come towards the final epochs. And now we are entering into the sixth of seven epochs, it means that towards the end of this current epoch, the fifth, we can see glimmers of what is coming. Individuals are experiencing breakthroughs, which more and more, start to ripple into the collective. The algorithms, the basic machinery of the whole thing, start to be revealed, and we see through the veil. That is what is happening now on this Earth.

More and more people are seeing through the veil, remembering their past lives and perhaps even the thread of where they are going next, and that the whole storyline of incarnation is that we are not individuals. We are not even constellations and families, but one being, one family, the human family.

The end of incarnation itself is coming and a new human will arrive here on this planet. 'A new heaven and a new earth', and a new kind of form is on its way. All the hierarchies of nature are bound up in this as well, because we cannot be separated from Gaia. We are an aspect of Gaia, and so for us to change, the whole of Gaia has to change. Animals, insects, minerals, plants, everything is caught up in this shift. That is why we see cataclysmic shifts occurring such as global warming, and different signs of the whole having its birth-death pangs.

I say this so that, hopefully, you may feel at ease rather than worried by the state of affairs on our planet. It has to go through this shift and we have to go through this change, this purification. It is always that way and it is embedded in our myths. It is a paradigm leap to another dimension, to a new kind of human being born, a collective human that knows what it is. They are aware of their interconnectivity with all nature, not just intellectually but in the physical cells of the body, and in every part of their being knows there is no way they could harm another. They would think, '*Why would I do that when I feel so good? Why would I harm another being? Why would I do that, when I know that other being is me? I can't possibly do it. I can't.*'

That is what is coming. A wonderful tale, isn't it?

YOUR TIMELESS TRAJECTORY
REINCARNATION AND REBIRTH – PART 5

Everything is moving and everything is turning. The earth rotates on its axis and around the Sun, which is rotating around the galactic core, which is also spinning and rotating around some other distant, supermassive black hole or other core. Everything is spinning and moving, and when you have forward momentum and spin, you have a spiral. All of life is a spiral, and incarnation is a spiral.

Cellular life imprints itself in seven-year cycles. There are many other cycles, but the seven-year cycle is deeply embedded into our cellular structure. Every seven years, we go around our own inner sun, and we repeat the cycle until we die. The interesting part is that when something happens in one of your seven-year cycles, it is a repeat of an earlier pattern at the same moment and stage in an earlier cycle.

Think of a major event in your life and when it appeared in your cycle. How old were you? Which seven-year cycle was it in? Which stage of that cycle was it in? In my own life, shortly after my eighth birthday I was sent away to boarding school and it was a terrible time. It was a profound shock around the beginning of my second seven-year cycle. It meant that I would have been imprinted with that shock seven years before, in the same place in my first seven-year cycle, and I have been re-imprinted with that shock again every seven years.

At the same point in each cycle, at the ages of 8, 15, 22, 29 and so on, something huge has shaken my life, not always a shock, but always some huge opportunity. In 1996, when I was twenty-nine, at the same moment in my seven-year cycle as I was sent to boarding school, I had my first massive mystical experience.

For three days in the summer of that year I was shaken to the depths of my reality. What I learned was that the wounding we receive is deeply connected to the awakening that we go through, and there are times in our lives when we enter portals of potential deeper misery or deeper healing, and events synchronise around us. We don't often notice it, but cellular life on this planet is deeply and mind-blowingly rhythmic. You could try looking into your own life and see if you can find the pivotal moments in your seven-year cycles.

We incarnate because of our *sanskaras*, our unfinished wound opportunities, and this opens up the idea that these seven-year cycles go beyond a single lifetime. So the same rhythms were operating in your last life and your lives before that too. The themes are passed on in perfect timing, so every shock or awakening is an equal distance apart and in succession. Our trajectory through time and space is dictated by these karmic patterns and the periods in which these shocks rock us, and we have to open to them, as deeper toxins come to the surface and we flush them through. We then have a period of integration before the next shock comes and there are tremors and smaller shock waves within the frame of the greater ones. It is all a beautifully-orchestrated pattern of pain, release and freedom.

What really blows me away is how deeply embedded these patterns are in our human biology. The body records everything like a Hall of Records, and all those thousands of past incarnations are imprinted in our DNA. I assume they are encoded in the non-coding DNA, which scientists used to refer to as junk DNA because they did not know how to read it. There are figures that suggest that up to 99% of our DNA is non-coding or junk DNA, and only a fraction of our DNA is actually about building and maintaining the body. The rest is storage, just like a computer.

Our body is a perfect map of the workings of the universe, and is the most efficient space-saving piece of bio-machinery that there is. What we don't understand we tend to think must be junk, but thousands of incarnations are recorded in that DNA, all memories encoded in a fractal form and stored hyper-efficiently. It would take a fractal computer (which we don't have yet) to unravel and decipher all those sequences, because they are not laid out neatly like ordinary DNA.

The only way to download those past memories is to access heightened states of consciousness beyond the Mental Plane, which most people are not yet capable of. Then you can understand the fractal layers and access them with a higher mind. However, I am not suggesting that we do that. I am suggesting that our journey, our trajectory through time and space, the past, the present and the future, is encoded in our bodies.

It is a huge thought that we are a living library, that we are following our trajectory in every life and we carry the whole weight of our incarnative past with us, and not just our own but that of the whole species. It is as if we are a great sinuous river. We begin high in the mountains, as a spring in some distant, lonely past and then we start living all these lives, these trickles, tributaries and waterfalls, until we come down and become a river in the plains. There we are joined by all the other streams and rivers that flow into ours, and the more evolved our journey becomes, the more we realise that we merge with the journeys of others. Then we come to the incarnations at the delta, the river mouth where the water is full of sediment, and it is stirred up and confused until it is cleansed in the ocean where, finally, we all become one.

Right now, you are probably in the phase when all the different rivers are flowing into yours. This means that you are a little more evolved than the young stream in the mountains.

When you are more evolved you have more karma, because there are more rivers joining yours down on the plains. As you approach the ocean things will become more intense and cloudy, yet at the same time lighter, with a huge rushing sense of anticipation that you are getting closer. To finally reach the ocean, we have to take in all that karma and transmute it for the sake of the whole.

Many of us would like to believe that we are coming to the end soon, that this is our last incarnation. I hear that a lot, but it is not very likely. One's final incarnation is one of utter glory and matchless splendour. Your consciousness becomes pure, like a diamond, and you will not be dealing with heaviness. You will be 'packing away your things' and working on the subtlest strings of the ego, those tiny fibres of separation become visible in the vast light that you are accessing.

I think it is good to be realistic, because there can be pressure, particularly from the Eastern teachings, an urgency to complete our evolution now. But why the rush after all these thousands of incarnations? We are coming finally towards the end and I think that, rather than rushing, the opposite is needed. Slow down, linger, make it last and squeeze the juice out of these final incarnations. They are going to be heavenly and at the same time bittersweet. We are finally surrendering our ego, and the whole theatre is changing. A vast change in the script is opening up the world. These next incarnations could be the most amazing of all as the Maya itself begins to quiver and dissolve. This is not the act that you want to miss.

So I suggest that you give yourself time and be gentle with yourself. What's the hurry? There is no need to rush at the finishing line. It is not a race, so slow down and drift in the currents, which are going to take us to the ocean anyway.

More and more advanced souls will be needed in the coming generations, and so, in the light of all this, I invite you to contemplate your own trajectory. Consider even where you would like to reincarnate next. Play with the idea. What do you need to complete in this life in order for the next life to be a life of utter freedom? This is the kind of view I want to encourage, and it seems inherently healthy to me. There is no need for an intense rush to get it all over, and it is just good to just be. Just being is the very thing that actually brings the end sooner. The paradox is that by slowing down we will actually get there sooner. And when we do get there and we are in between lives and out of form, time as we know it will not exist.

There is a level now where we may choose what we truly want our life to be, but we are not choosing from our ego but from the depths of our soul. So think about what your ideal life looks like and dream that in. It is the very life that is encoded for you. This is the other paradox, that the life we feel we are dreaming up is actually the one that is predestined.

So trust in your trajectory and the trajectories of others, and those you love, because there is a perfection to it all. Reincarnation is a trajectory through time and space. Death is perfectly timed, and it is a place as well as a time, because everything is moving. We have to arrive at that place, the whirlpool opens and we pass through it into another birth. Probably we have a pause in between, in the Bardos, and then once again we emerge and we are born. But soon we are going to be coming into a new world with new bio-vehicles, with upgrades that will allow us to do things we cannot even imagine. We will become conscious of all this in our new form, as we remember our past lives and view our trajectory, and those of others, clearly. This is all coming: the time of resolution and the time of miracles.

You need not fear your death. So rather than giving in to any fears you may have around it, try to relax and participate in its arrival and accept its perfection. As others depart around the world, be with them with this sense of adventure, freedom and perspective. Even though death can be terrifying and filled with pain, it can also be filled with great gentleness, compassion and grace.

So let's not rush into our awakening. Pause, be contemplative, be a creative witness. Let life slide easily into death, and death back into life. We can participate in this creation, surrender and just let it flow. There is no urgency to awaken and no need for hours of meditation with a frown on your face. That will not get you there.

We can long for our freedom, and the longing is important, but let it be balanced through pacing, rhythm, acceptance and deep, timeless patience.

PREPARATION FOR DYING
– THE REBIRTH SEQUENCE

In a way, all of life is a preparation for death. The Rebirth Sequence is how to prepare for the transition. It is a teaching and a powerful contemplation for those who are preparing for death, but it is also a teaching for everyone. Death and rebirth are woven into life and our everyday reality. There will be times when we are called to surrender something of ourselves, perhaps when we are going through some kind of initiation, turning point or crisis. It might be the death of someone close, or it could be any of the many processes that we have to move through during major changes in our lives. So this sequence is applicable to everyone.

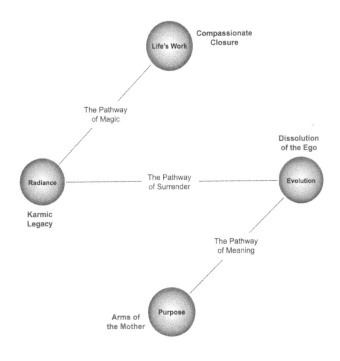

THE REBIRTH SEQUENCE

The Rebirth Sequence goes through four stages and it is one of Involving. If you know the Gene Keys and my teachings you will recognise that it is in a way a reverse of the Activation Sequence, which is one of Evolving. The Gene Keys that make up the Rebirth Sequence, your Life's Work, Radiance, Evolution and Purpose, are codes and archetypes specific to you, taken from your Gene Keys Profile. The sequence involves us at the deepest level in creation as we learn to surrender more and more deeply to all that is and to the perfection of the sequence itself, and to trust in every stage of our life journey, even the very final stages. These are things that we can take deeply into contemplation.

The first stage, relates to our Life's Work Gene Key, which is about what we are here to do, and is about closure – Compassionate Closure. Depending on what the nature of your Life's Work is, at some point you will reach a stage when it is time to bring it to an end. And when our Life's Work ends, we leave. That is the nature of what we are here for. As soon as we have finished our work, we move on.

Compassionate Closure is about considering the people whom you are leaving and what you are leaving behind, and doing the necessary things to make it as easy for them as possible before you leave and make the Grand Transition. Then, instead of thinking only of yourself (which obviously you will) you bring things to a compassionate close.

The first thing to consider is, *'What am I leaving behind?'* and *'How can I make it as easy as possible for those whom I leave behind?'* Spend some time with those questions.

Compassionate Closure can also be applied to other transitions or situations. If it was the end of a relationship, you would look at *'How can I bring this to a close in a gracious way that leaves a good feeling for those involved or, at least, within me?'* In that way, you will have done your absolute utmost to be of service to the situation, to your partner and to anyone else involved.

It is not always possible to bring it to a Compassionate Closure, because sometimes you don't know how the other person is feeling or how the situation really is, and there might be a lot of discomfort or pain. In that case, do it for yourself, even just inside yourself sometimes, and make sure that you have done all the external things that you need to. Then you have finished with it in the best way possible, thinking of others who are going to be affected. Compassionate Closure means thinking about the practicalities.

The way we die can actually propel us forward in evolution, even if we have had a very difficult life, or even if we have had a kind of selfish life. Or it may be that it has been a life of struggle and you feel you have not done what you really could have done, and not really lived your Life's Work, for whatever reason. In any case, at the very end, bring it to a gracious close. It is possible to make huge advances spiritually at the end, because there is so much potential for transformation then.

The second stage in the sequence is your Karmic Legacy. In the Gene Keys Hologenetic Profile, it relates to what is called your Radiance, which is beautiful, because your Karmic Legacy radiates out behind you after you have gone. Your Karmic Legacy is in how you bring things to a close. If you can do it on the surface in a compassionate way, that is wonderful, but consider also what else you will be leaving behind.

Your Karmic Legacy, your Radiance, is everything that you have ever said and done, your entire presence. Your legacy is not only your work and the nice things that you might leave behind – perhaps you are a writer and you will be leaving a good book or two behind! But your legacy is really about the joy that you have created in others, in their hearts, through the words that you have spoken, through all the good things you have done.

Although we might look back and think, *'I could have done a lot more good things,'* your Karmic Legacy is about *'How much goodness can I leave behind me at the end? How many things can I do?'* It's not just *'What can I give away on the surface?'* but, rather, *'What is the most I can really give of my spirit at the end?'* It might be as simple as asking someone for forgiveness, or forgiving someone. It does not even have to be done formally. It can be done in your heart, because your Radiance is something that is magical. This is the Pathway of Magic.

You cannot really see your Karmic Legacy, although you might get a sense of it if you were to be at your own funeral, as you would hear what people were saying, and feel what was inside their hearts as they remembered you. Essentially, your Karmic Legacy is something magical which is created out of all the good words and deeds you have said and done throughout your life. Every act we make and every word and tone we use have a frequency embedded in them, and they endure eternally and spread throughout the universe.

Our acts live in eternity. That is quite something to consider! What is your Karmic Legacy? Even if you are young and at the beginning of your life, it is something to think about.

You can build an amazing field of radiance through how you live, how you speak and how you think. Consider if the thoughts you have are kind and forgiving. Are you able to yield to life's initiations or do you try to resist them? How much can you grow and learn, soften and be kind? How much benevolence can you radiate during the course of one life, or during the course of one hour? Really consider every act as sacred. That is the foundation of the Magical Universe.

Every act lives in eternity and every word is a sacred word which will vibrate eternally. This is the whole nature of karma, the karma that we leave behind, our Karmic Legacy.

After the karma has begun to emanate into the cosmos, and at the end we have placed the crowning glory of our Karmic Legacy – what we have done, words we have spoken or things we have left behind – comes the third stage in the sequence, the Dissolution of the Ego. It happens particularly as we approach death and it begins to happen automatically. Our identity begins to detach from the vehicle that it is housed in, our attachment to the form. And in the same way that we arrive through a nine-month-sequence, we leave through a nine-month-sequence, whether we are aware of that or not. It is indeed a mystery.

The detaching and dissolution of the ego relates to our Evolution Gene Key. We have to surrender and the Pathway of Surrender is a very magical and extraordinary thing.

The Dissolution of the Ego is a magical event, and any transition can bring it about to some degree. You will be called upon to surrender your position in some way, and this allows your ego to dissolve. It could be that a little bit of the ego is dissolved or, if it is right at the end, the whole thing dissolves, all of the false identity that believes that it is separate, a body, a name and a separate being. Everyone who is dying goes through this at some level, because it is a process engaged in our brain and our being. It involves profound surrender. This is not ending our evolution but shifting it to another plane, and it is the closure of our external physical evolution in this life.

When there is a major transition in our lives, an initiation of some sort, many people tend to resist it. What we are really called upon to do is to surrender our ego, our individual viewpoint, our attachment to the outcome and how we want it to look, and yield to a force that is greater than us, of which we are also a part. Any transition that you are moving through in your life can hold the same grain of truth, in that you are invited to surrender some deep aspect of your identification with something, and, as you let go, you find more and more freedom.

Surrender is a journey of layers, and moving through them hurts, especially at the beginning. But as we deepen our surrender, and our ego lets go, it becomes so sweet it is almost blissful as we surrender into the fourth and final stage of the process.

The last stage is the Pathway of Meaning and it relates to our Purpose Gene Key. It brings us the final, deeper meaning and purpose of our lives, as we are surrendering into the Arms of the Beloved or the Arms of the Mother, the Mother's embrace. The Mother is the divine space, the void at the heart of all things, and it is not an empty void, but a loving space. We become one with the Mother's embrace and have to surrender everything, and just fall into the arms of that mystery at the core of life. We fall into an aching, beautiful, endless, eternal mystery. Some call it God or the Divine.

I call it the Divine Mother because it is the essence of tenderness and love. It is what we feel and experience and what we know and remember as we surrender and dissolve. The Mother's embrace welcomes us. It is a fathomless mystery. As we make the final sacrifice and give up our identity, we receive the gifts. We become one with the Great One, the True Self. It is the final letting go into the arms of the Mother.

And whether you subscribe to this or not, at some level it is also a recycling and a renewal. Every death is a rebirth. Which is why I call this the Rebirth Sequence.

We are either reborn in another eternal dimension, or we are reborn here, again, on this planet Gaia. We have a trajectory that we follow, and our rebirth brings us literally into the womb and the arms of another mother. It is a sequence that the Tibetans call Bardo. The stages are very clear, and there is a lot of letting go. Eventually we arrive in another womb and are reborn in another life bringing our Karmic Legacy with us. The reverberations of what we leave in one life imprint the next. It is a beautiful teaching.

There comes a time, if we have completed entirely and our business here is finished, which is a rare thing on this plane, when we surrender and the ego dissolves. We surrender into a higher dimension and enter a wider life, wider than we can possibly imagine or put into words. That is an even greater mystery. One of the things we are going to experience in this process is the letting go of layers of fear, which is what this sequence is here to do. As we consider it now, we realise that as we are growing and evolving, we are also dying. We are moving towards death all the time and this is not a negative thing. We are being asked to surrender, every day, deeper and deeper into the mystery of life.

If you are near the end of your life and you are considering these things, consider what your legacy is, and how to close things with grace so that you can make this beautiful journey, dropping layers of fear, desire and identity, as you surrender into the arms of the Mother.

CHAPTER 6

RIPPLES OF CONSCIOUSNESS

When we learn about a new philosophy or technique,
or we hear a story that alters our view of things,
something shifts within our consciousness
and it can ripple right through our core,
out to our friends and families, to our
wider circle and beyond to the collective.

These moments of realisation have the power
to open us and shift our way of being,
and ultimately can change the world.

MELTING THE MALE EGO
AND REWILDING THE SOUL

I have been learning about rewilding, not in the ecological sense, but as a philosophy and a way of looking at things in life. This I have learned mostly through my wife, in the way she approaches nature in the garden and life around our community. She is a wildlife warden and she approaches it all in a very feminine, intuitive way. I didn't understand it for a long time, but I am now finally beginning to get it.

We have a beautiful lawn at the back of our house, and the seat where I sit and contemplate in the morning overlooks the lawn, with the garden framed in the background. It is a village garden, which we both love, and we love gardening. I have always taken pride in my lawn (as many men stereotypically do) and enjoyed getting the lawnmower out, keeping the grass looking neat and tidy and creating a nice place to hang out. But over the last few years we decided to stop cutting it, and instead let the lawn grow and rewild. I cut some paths so you could get through to the gate, but essentially we just let it grow into wild, long, ragged grasses, herbs and weeds, whatever came up.

We have been watching this process for a few years. I sit out there at sunrise to do my contemplative practice, drink my tea and gaze at the world in front of me, and I have noticed a huge increase in life, particularly bird life. Many birds come in, as they love the long grasses and they flutter around in them because of all the insects there. This increase in diversity is attracting more and more birds and we are watching the wildlife returning.

So, I have let go of my nice, neat lawn and the slightly controlling aspect that we humans sometimes have in how we want everything to look neat and tidy. Because, sometimes, in trying to make things look neat and tidy we lose touch with nature, which is not neat and tidy, but has a wild harmony.

My wife is also mindful in how she approaches the vegetable garden. You might look at our vegetable patch and think it looks really messy, like the lawn, and yet when you look at it, it is filled with life. Some vegetables have been left to self-seed and flower in the autumn and some of them have jumped across into the flower beds, and some of the flowers have crossed over to the vegetable beds, and other things have arrived that have been brought by birds or other wildlife.

Whatever likes growing has been encouraged, the weeds as well, so the garden is pretty wild. Big, tangly, difficult weeds like brambles and those that choke other flowers and plants are taken out, but low-level weeds are allowed because they hold the moisture in the soil, so it doesn't make sense to pull them all out. For years, I would say, *'Can't I just weed that?'* and my wife would say, *'No, no, leave them, because they retain the moisture and attract more insects.'* And I realised that she is right. If you pull all the weeds out you are left with bare earth, and what is that really for, but our need for it to look tidy?

Many vegetable gardens have a very neat look with all the weeds taken out and everything growing in nice tidy rows with lots of bare soil in between, which looks impressive. Our vegetable garden is a kind of jungle with vegetables and flowers growing randomly all over the place, but it is just as productive, if not more, and it has a greater diversity of creatures, insects and birds.

In the early days, I thought it looked messy with things growing haphazardly here and there. And some things don't do as well as others, but then they fade out, and eventually everything starts to bloom and flourish where it is through its own process. It is organic in that way. Not just organic in that we don't use any synthetic fertilisers or sprays, it is organic because it has created its own wild ecosystem.

This has taken me a while to understand. I have had to let my left-brain, male ego melt, that ego that wants to control and have things looking neat, tidy and organised, and, in fact, our garden is quite organised, but it is a wild organising. The right-brained, feminine side in us isn't obsessed with things looking perfect, and it operates in a softer, more yielding, more pliant way. It is much more trusting and it takes more risks, and I love that. There is an uncertainty around it all, because you never quite know what is going to come next or where, and you don't have to excessively plan. You can do some initial planning, but nature has a plan of its own, which is extraordinary and wonderful. When I sit in the garden now, I am amazed at how much life there is to look at that was not there before.

I would like to invite you to look at this inside yourself, inside your life. That male ego is not just in men. I know plenty of women who have a strong male ego. It is the left side of the brain that likes order, control and organisation, but in a linear way, and there is nothing wrong with that. But, from what I am learning, the perfect balance in an ecosystem is not 50-50. If you know the Gene Keys, you will know that Equilibrium is Gene Key 50, the halfway point to a hundred. But a perfect balance in an ecosystem requires less structure and more wildness, probably something like 66% wildness and 33% structure and form, (though I am intuiting those figures with my right brain).

You can apply that ratio to most things in life, to relationships, parenting or business. If you have too much of the linear, male-planning structure stuff, it will throttle the wildness and naturalness, which then will not be able to thrive and flourish. Try applying it to your relationships, your partner, your friends, your family, and let go of some of that need for things to look and feel and be the way your ego would like them to be. It might be that we would like to control someone's behaviour in some way and for them to be a much more neatly-clipped garden. *'Can't you just clip those things, those traits in your nature, and tidy them up?'*

Of course, there are certain traits, like big, thick invasive weeds, that must be dealt with because they are self-destructive, and hopefully they are dealt with in diplomatic, kind, honest and transparent ways. There are other behaviours, however, that we could let go of a little in the desire to have perfect relationships. If we could yield a bit more, when we see that person behaving in that way, and allow them to have those traits that make it a bit messy between us, then we will be moving more towards the feminine, soft approach of kindness.

I do not mean that women are soft, because this is not about gender. (Some people might look at it the other way round and see the feminine as fierce and the masculine as soft.) I am referring to the poles inside us that Jung called *Animus* and *Anima*. Too much of the masculine, male pole, linear, left-brain anywhere in our lives causes strangulation and resentment, and stagnation in business, due to communication problems and relational problems. Those areas in a business, an ecosystem, or any natural system are the feminine parts, the relational parts, and the parts that flow, and they need greater attention. But the structure, the form, the planning and the organisation are needed much less to achieve balance.

The right brain doesn't look at things in a logical, linear way. It thrives with a little more chaos, with a little more looseness and wildness. Right-brain living is about melting the harder, more opinionated side of our personality, and our need for order, which is a huge thing when you start applying it to all areas of your life. The art of contemplation can help you see what you need to let go of, and where you need to yield and soften your approach, whether it is a relationship, a person, an opinion or a view of life.

Many people say that they are very 'right brain', but the reality is when you apply the process of right-brain, non-linear thinking, you discover that it is not really about thinking but more embodying the right brain by being it and living it, which is a huge thing because it changes the way you see and do things, and it is changing my views of life and reality deeply. The wiser someone becomes, the more yielding they become. They do not become more hard and stagnant, but become softer, like water. It is the wisdom of age, of something that becomes seasoned and wiser. This is a teaching of the Tao.

Try bringing flow and freedom into your work and life, with a smattering of organisation and planning. Go easy on yourself and others. Let your ego dissolve a bit and see how things can soften. Yield and go with the flow of life and nature. Rewild your soul.

OCEAN OF STABILITY

I was once coming home from a retreat, driving along the wild coastline of Devon. It was a beautiful evening and I stopped to clamber down to a secluded beach. I sat there watching the sun on the waves and listening to the sea birds screeching overhead. It was a beautiful experience. I could see a small pinnacle of rock out in the sea, and I decided to head out to it. So I got into my wetsuit and swam out into quite a big swell, aware that there was some risk in being alone in this wild place, with tides and currents that I was not familiar with. Still, I swam out to the rock, climbed onto it and sat on top.

The waves were washing over my legs, but my top half was mostly above the water. I got myself comfortable, and as I was sitting there in that wild sea, it felt as though I was sitting on top of the water, and it must have looked like that too, if someone had been watching from the shore. It was an extraordinary feeling. I closed my eyes and I went into the deep space of the allegory of the situation I found myself in, because it was exactly like life. These were the stormy waters, the unpredictable waves that can wash over us and perhaps sometimes threaten to take us away. Yet I could feel a connection through my base, through my core, right down into the earth, through the sea and through the rock that came up through the ocean, to me, sitting on top.

I felt a beautiful stability, even though everything on the surface was moving and changing. It was a deep, unchanging solidity at the core of who I was. I closed my eyes and even when large waves washed over me and came right up to my chest, I felt completely safe on that rock because I felt the gravity, the stability. It made me think about my life, what

I do, who I am, and the Gene Keys, and I realised that stability is what I am bringing through the Gene Keys, through these teachings.

Many people who come into the Gene Keys on the Golden Path programme find a core connection to their higher purpose. That purpose is not what you are here to do, but is a sense of being which the doing emerges out of. And until you have a deep, ongoing connection to that sense of higher purpose, you will not be able to truly connect with the base of who you are, with the base of life, and you will not ever truly feel stable.

Whatever comes to you in the world, whatever life throws at you, whatever challenges you meet, if you have that base of core stability, then you will be able to weather it with grace, and be able to deal with any storm. Starting with that sense of deep core stability, which comes from knowing and having contacted the purpose of your life in this world, is the foundation of all higher questing for truth. Although that higher purpose will vary for each of us, it will be some form of love or service. The style of it and how we feel it inside will be different for everyone, but its essence is always love.

The Gene Keys offer us reflection and ongoing contemplation so that we can contact that stability. We live in tempestuous times, and even though the world is relatively peaceful when we look at it historically, it can feel that things around us are collapsing on the outside. The systems we have designed and built are showing themselves not to be fit for purpose, and that means that there are uncertain times ahead.

The indications are that what we have built is beginning to decay, fall apart and crumble, and on the outside this means we are moving through a period of intense change. On the inside, the currents of internal connection to the source of being are brighter and perhaps more available than ever. So it is a wonderful time to engage on an inner journey, since the conditions are perfect for it.

You often see this in the world, that something on the outside is going one way and something on the inside is going the other. This seems to be a universal law. On the inside, there is an ascension and an opening, and on the outside there is a falling apart.

I would expect, although, not wanting to be a doom-monger, that the falling apart will continue in the years ahead in the world. The outside will feel a less safe place, but on the inside the world can feel safer and safer as we make these connections. We can navigate the changes, which are all beneficial in the long run, from a place of core stability in our physical bodies, families, communities, emotions, heart and spirit.

I want to give you the sense of what it is like to sit on that rock and feel that deep anchor to the core of your life purpose. When you begin to contact that feeling, it can really begin to change your life.

THE BACKBONE OF TRUTH

To have a strong, supple spine is directly connected to how we embody truth in our lives. To stand out, upright and proud, and to move with grace, agility, flexibility and with majesty, are all attributes of a strong backbone in your life.

Your backbone can be many things, but it has to have a central anchor, which is your vision, your goal, your spiritual, pure essence, your insight, your *sadhana*, your daily discipline to move towards Christ, to move towards the ultimate. My wish is to set aside the jargon of the spiritual path and to bring us back to the essential core of the backbone of truth. Speak the truth. Know the truth. See the truth. These are simple, timeless practices that can transform our lives. Even if you have physical or karmic challenges with your spine, you can still show a strong backbone in your life. In many ways, even more so.

So stand proud, not with the vain pride of the ego, but with the pride of the sun, of aliveness, of vitality. As best as you can, sing out with the pride of this beautiful form, this body that we inhabit. That is what we are here to do. And be disciplined, as you have to have some inner discipline in your life that is constant, that is always working towards the infinite, the eternal. This is what gives us the backbone we truly need, something we can consistently rely on inside ourselves, supporting us like a great tree.

Our spine is like the great trunk of the eternal tree, which sucks the power of the earth up through its cambium and then spreads out through our vision and our mind, out into the cosmos. That balance of the tree is the balance of our spine, that central column. Try to bring light into the links of your spine, through subtle movements or through meditation, from the sacrum and the pelvis, working your way up all the links to the cranium.

The spiral moves up and down the spine, beautiful and releasing, with the different energies that wrap around it in the serpent path, the *kundalini*. It brings in that essence of the glory, the majesty and the silence that we are into the links of the spine, giving us stability, power and humility.

Bring light, awareness and love into your spine. Bring truth into your spine.

THE VOIDNESS OF YOUR INTELLECT IS BUDDHAHOOD

'The voidness of your intellect is Buddhahood' is a phrase that is taken from 'The Tibetan Book of the Dead'. What does it really mean?

We are thinking beings. We think we are this body and we think we are our thoughts. We believe this and we take it for granted. At some point, though, we may wonder if there is more to this human experience. Many mystics and sages have spoken of higher realms, of the space beyond the mind, or of the light *behind* the mind and *within* the mind. But maybe we don't believe in such expanded states and we put it down to an idealistic possibility, or something that perhaps only certain people have access to. So how do we attain it?

The mind can connect you to everything. Yet for most of us the mind separates us from everything. It anchors us into this human package and gives us a unique way of thinking, one which we may pride ourselves upon, since it can give rise to sharp and powerful intellects. But, even with the highest IQ, unless you have experienced, even for a moment, a state beyond the mind, it can be difficult to truly understand a phrase like *'The voidness of your intellect is Buddhahood'*.

What was before the beginning, before the big bang? What is infinity? The thinking mind alone cannot penetrate these questions. The thinking mind is very different from the infinite mind. The logical mind cannot grasp the concept of infinity, so it wraps it up in circular thinking. Infinity is a truth, infinity is a paradox that logic cannot encompass.

Mysteries like this can be experienced only with your full being, accessing the higher, wider planes beyond the mind, and this requires meditation, prayer or other disciplines that take you beyond your own thinking. Then, in time, you may glimpse a spark of the eternal light of consciousness that lies there, and experience the ecstasy that can pour through your being when you see with the clarity that shines through.

Contemplate that possibility over and over in your life. Open your mind to all possibilities and learn to think innocently again. Having opinions and forming judgments is part of being human, but try to hold them lightly, and recognise the validity of all perspectives. Otherwise you could become trapped in closed worldviews that keep you isolated and locked in mental paradigms that shut you away and disconnect you from others.

Buddhahood means to be fully self-realised, and to know that the mind is everything. The Buddhists negate the mind with words like 'voidness', but you might also read this as its opposite – as 'everythingness'. It is the same thing. There is nowhere the mind is not, and nowhere the mind stops. It is infinite.

'The voidness of your intellect is Buddhahood'. If you keep an open mind, one day you will understand what this means.

 # EASY IS RIGHT

The well-known Chinese sage, Chuang Tzu said many wise things, but perhaps the wisest words he ever spoke were, *'Easy is right.'* Contained in these three words is a vast philosophy, which is what I love about Eastern mystics.

When I was a student at university, I studied what Westerners call 'Philosophy', but my main interest was to balance it with Eastern philosophy, which is completely different. Eastern philosophy condenses massive bodies of understanding into quintessences, and leaves it to you to figure out what it really means. You can only work out these things by living them, which is why the great sages like Lao Tzu spoke in such condensed words and phrases that yet have so many layers of meaning. There are also many different interpretations that can be drawn from their original characters drawn in Mandarin.

If you contemplate those three simple words, *'easy is right'*, and open them up to see what is inside, you can find dimensions to be explored and whole universes contained within them. What can be written on these pages is tiny in comparison. To the best of my ability, I have made a great part of my life revolve around *'easy is right'*. Try taking those three words into your life and see what happens. Really explore them and see how you can apply them to any practical problems you have right now. See how 'easy is right' can change your difficulties and open them up, as well as softening the hard edges of your life.

'Easy is right' can be misunderstood, though. Sometimes you come to an obstacle or a blockage in your path in life, and you have a choice to tackle the obstacle or to walk away. If

you follow *easy is right* you might think the answer is to walk away. But if you took that attitude to everything, you would miss many great opportunities, and the potential for all sorts of transformations in your life. So there is a subtlety to *easy is right* because sometimes the path is not easy, but it is right.

Easy does not mean comfortable. It is not the same. You may decide if it feels right and if you have the courage, you may decide to tackle the obstacle head-on and lean into it, instead of rushing away because it is something that you don't want to deal with. If you decide to deal with the obstacle, then you have the opportunity to go through a transformational experience, which could be very uncomfortable. But if you give yourself to it a hundred percent, you will unlock its transformational magic. You will realise that the thing that took you forwards, that sense of *'this is correct'*, actually led you through a portal, and now you have transformed something that won't haunt you again.

It is a fundamental truth that when we are completely authentic inside ourselves, then we move through experiences with ease. Although such experiences may even cause us intense discomfort and pain, we can still be in the flow of ease and feel that it is right. At other times, we may come to those decision points and see that there is a way around the obstacle, but still decide to turn away from it, as the correct thing would be just to avoid it. That would also be in the flow of *'easy is right'*.

So, the powerful wisdom in *'easy is right'* can also be subtle. Until you come to a decision point, you won't know which is the best way to go. And there are no good and bad ways, there is only you discovering the easy way and the difficult way.

Something to consider is that the Western mind loves the difficult way. The more difficult and complicated it looks, the more we trust it. The simpler it looks, the more cautious we are.

We think that it just can't be that simple. Yet, the really deep truths of life and the principles of the universe are beautifully simple. They may spiral out into infinite complexities, but the core principles are simple, beautiful and exquisite.

'Easy is right' is really more about living poetically than it is about solving things. Our modern, westernised mindset is set on figuring things out; *'What's my purpose? I'm going to figure it out. I'm going to go on a long Gene Keys course to figure it all out. I'm going to read that big, complex Gene Keys book 'Embracing Your Higher Purpose'.*

The thinking is that because something is so intricate and complex it must be true. Which in a sense, is a trick, because what I regard as my masterpiece is a very small book, less than a hundred pages long, called 'The Art of Contemplation'. But if I went round suggesting that people read this little book that I wrote, only a few would be interested, because it seems too simple. Of course, I am not saying that the big, complex Gene Keys book is wrong, but part of the mind looks for the complex and creates complexity where there is simplicity.

As a teacher of the Gene Keys, and with the art of contemplation as my main teaching, I am asked many questions. Sometimes I reflect those questions back to each person, by pointing out that if you contemplate anything in enough depth, the answer will reveal itself to you (which some find infuriating). Contemplation activates physical, neurological and emotional pathways inside us, opening us up to the universal core wisdom in new ways. So, my answer to many questions is, *'Look within,'* because if I try to answer something for you, it won't necessarily answer you in a wholly satisfying way. It might give you a moment of insight or some inspiration, but if it hasn't come from your own revelation, it will not have a physical impact on your being.

So the only way you can really understand *easy is right* is to unlock it yourself.

A FIELD OF PLAY
– YOUR GENE KEYS PROFILE

If you are interested in the Gene Keys, one of the things you may have discovered is your Hologenetic Profile. You may already be journeying with it on many levels, because a whole playground has been opened up in which to explore these profiles. But what if your profile were wrong? What if your parents had given you the wrong birth time or date, and you were exploring a profile that wasn't related to your birth time at all?

This is a particularly interesting scenario for me to contemplate, because I had that experience when I was involved in another system, Human Design, and it turned out that for many years I was working with the wrong birth time. Then, one day, my father came across an old diary which had my correct birth time recorded in it, so I redid my chart, and it turned out that, according to Human Design, I was a completely different kind of person. Discovering the details of my Human Design Bodygraph the first time, and thinking about myself in a certain way had already changed the reality of the person I thought I was. Then, with the correction of my birth time and my chart, my reality changed all over again. But it actually double-changed my reality, because, at that point, I began to let go a little bit and start playing with the structure of my Human Design.

I want to apply the same thing to the Gene Keys, and so I want to encourage you to hold your Hologenetic Profile lightly, and play with it. This does not mean discarding it, or seeing it as incorrect. There are alignments embedded deep in the Hologenetic Profile that have a specific resonance to us because of when and where we were born. And there is a real authenticity in that, especially when you can really recognise the patterns in the profile, but it is also important not to get fixated on it.

Even though the Hologenetic Profile came to me, and I pioneered it and sent it out to the world, when I am asked questions about the detail of the mechanics of it, surprising as it may be to those who ask, I mostly don't know the answers. I have to use my intuition to discover what the answer is, and you can do the same thing. It is a playground for us to explore, and at a certain point, when the resonance of those higher frequencies has become deeply embedded in us, we can let the profile go. It is important to keep that in mind. At the beginning, dive deep into it. Identify with it, play with it, learn from it, explore it, share it. But remember that one day you can let it go.

You don't actually have to follow the Hologenetic Profile, which, based on your specific birth details, tells you x, y and z. In fact, the entire field of all 64 Gene Keys is available inside us. Another way into the Gene Keys, into the matrix, is the through the Dream Arc, which is a Gene Keys programme that invites you in through the animal realm. Each Gene Key is related to an animal, bird or insect. So if there is a particular animal that you are interested in or feel drawn to, you can find your path in through that creature. Something that I have always felt attracted to and that shows up a lot for me is the dragonfly. I love dragonflies. I often dream about them and have many pictures of them at home. The dragonfly is the symbol of the 55th Gene Key, and this has a deep and significant connection for me.

You may also have a special connection with a certain animal, and you might expect that to mean that you will also have a deep resonance with the corresponding Gene Key.

But if you find that it is not even in your profile, it doesn't matter. There are other ways into the matrix, and this is a reminder that we ought to hold it lightly as we explore it.

Something else to consider is when you say, *'I'm a this, I'm a that.'* We all have these different 'I ams', and rather than adding more, you could try saying, *'I'm drawn to...' or 'I have this theme in my life...'* of conflict, silence, addiction, peace, whatever it might be. Most importantly, hold it all lightly. Enjoy it, play with it, love it, and then let it go.

THE PEARL AND THE RELEASE OF MIRACLES

When you look at the Gene Keys Golden Path, you will see that the Pearl sits within the triangle that makes up the Pearl Sequence, and holds an exciting geometrical position within the whole, which is really significant and magical, in terms of how it relates to the sequence. The Pearl represents a finale, a culmination, a harvest, and in a way it is the crystallisation of the entire Golden Path. It also forms the nexus of an advanced expansion of the Pearl, called the Star Pearl.

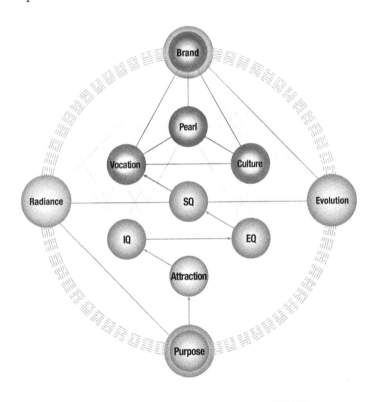

THE GOLDEN PATH AND THE PEARL SEQUENCE
(VOCATION, CULTURE, BRAND & PEARL)

When the Pearl Sequence originally came through to me as a transmission, as a download, it came to some extent merged with the Venus Sequence, although, as a sequence, I understood it slightly differently by interpreting it through the geometries. The position of Jupiter at the time of your birth dictates what your Pearl will be, which in Human Design terms is called the Conscious Jupiter. As an astrologer you might look at the position of the Pearl and make all kinds of interpretations, but without understanding all the other planetary activations and what they lead up to in the storyline, you won't fully comprehend what the Pearl really represents until you look at the whole sequence and how it relates to the narrative of your inner life and its evolution.

Having said that, I often tell people to not really bother looking at their Pearl. They do, though, because there it is, sitting in the middle of its triangle, and they want to know what it is. But when I say not to bother looking at it, I only say it half-jokingly because it only comes as the culmination of everything else and it is, in fact, a revelation and a conclusion.

Contemplating the Gene Key and the Line of your Pearl, you are really looking at the future and the finale of your journey of individuation. Although, on another level it is the present, because it is inside you, and even though you might be contemplating your future, you are contemplating it in the now. So you are radiating that energy, and it could give you something precious.

In the old days, I used to call the Pearl the 'Release of Miracles', and that is exactly what it is. It sits in the heart of a quantum web, with all the work you do in your Golden Path, the contemplative breakthroughs, the insights and the epiphanies leading to the crystallisation in the Pearl.

But, more than that, it all leads to a release of what we could call miracles, on multiple levels and dimensions of reality.

The process begins when you have attained an inner equilibrium through contemplating and treading the Golden Path. At which point, your sacred wound, the core, and your Vocation will start to shine, and you will be aligned with your Culture. Your Life's Work will be refined, so that everything fits beautifully. Your SQ will be shining and softening across your heart. Your Radiance will be flowering, and your Evolution inspiring you. Your EQ will be in balance with your IQ. Your Attractor field will be clean and magnetising the synchronicity field of your aura, and you will be anchored in your Purpose, having had those deep breakthroughs from your Activation Sequence and feeling that your challenge is something you embrace wholeheartedly. When all these things are balanced and humming along, then the Pearl begins to crystallise and dawn.

I like to say that the Pearl 'dawns', because it is a kind of trigger point for releasing miracles. The collective consciousness that the Pearl represents is a synchronicity field that is activated, and then situations, people and events that are connected to you through chains of dharma begin to unravel. It is an unravelling of the weave in the tapestry of your inner life, and your true dharma begins to unfold before your eyes. And it seems magical, because grace is touching all the different areas of your life and all the people that you are connected to. It travels through the fractal lines, opening up people and bringing them 'online', and opening doorways, possibilities and opportunities that had been waiting, but had been closed or dormant before.

So, when you look at your Pearl and its line, allow your intuition to travel into it and rest there. Feel the buzz and the vibration of what is waiting to open up, because there is a code in there that will release all those miracles. Something happens inside you for the code to be activated, but it isn't only activated within you, because through grace it will be unlocked around you too. Often this happens through others, in miraculous moments, forgivings, or whatever form they may take, and then all manner of magical currents and miracles are catalysed in your life by the Shadow, Gift, and Siddhi of the Pearl. When you enter this state of grace and higher harmony, as you will one day, the Pearl will be a very beautiful thing to contemplate.

HUMAN DESIGN

Many who have been drawn to explore the Gene Keys came to the Human Design system first, and perhaps found the Gene Keys through Human Design. If you are not already familiar with Human Design, I don't really recommend taking that path, because holding two transmissions can be a lot, or even too much. Unless, of course, you felt very drawn to Human Design, then absolutely follow that intuition. I came through Human Design and I entered into a very deep and involved study of it for seven years. It was an invaluable support in my journey, and it helped me understand many things that I simplified and adapted to become the Gene Keys.

Human Design is essentially a mental system. However, it allows your mind to relax so that you can enter more deeply into life, which is the reason for its being a mental system. What you do not get from Human Design is a lot of heart, as that is just not part of its remit.

The Human Design view of the world is one based on certainty. You find out that you are a certain type, with a particular authority and a strategy which are fixed by your time of birth, and if you follow the system everything that you do will be correct. I have a fundamental issue with that because if there is a way that is correct, there is also a way that is incorrect. This creates a dilemma, because it sets up a group of people who are doing things correctly, and conversely a group of people who are doing things incorrectly, and that can cause difficulty, exclusivity and cultism. That is the basic challenge that Human Design has, with all its wonder and esoteric, penetrating wisdom, and that is the fundamental flaw that has to be resolved somehow by each person travelling through that system.

It is the same with any system, since there is a fundamental flaw in every system, including the Gene Keys. But it is different for each person, because we have to resolve these flaws, these paradoxes inside us, and then move beyond them. The whole point is to allow the system to educate you, to inform you, to lead you deeper inside yourself and your being, to understand yourself and to understand others, and to be more compassionate. If the system you are using is not doing that, then it is of no value, as far as I am concerned. It has to create more compassion, understanding and ease in your life, which Human Design does for many people, so it is valid in that sense.

We need to be careful with all systems, with anything we read or hear that is written or spoken by another, including me. We have to assimilate and filter it through our own intuition. We also have to trust in the inherent alignment that we feel to the teaching and the teacher. If we trust it, that is enough, and it will lead us in the right direction. The key to following any teaching or any teacher, or anything is to listen to your attunement to that person, that statement, that truth. It is all in the cadence and the tone. That is how we truly know when something is correct.

PERSON FIRST, NUMBERS SECOND

Systems such as the Enneagram, the Human Design System and the Gene Keys all involve numbers, formulas and categorisation to create some kind of profile. For me there is a golden rule with such things, and that is *person first, numbers second.* It is a really important rule and not following it is a mistake that many people make.

Whether you are looking at numerology, astrology or another similar system, it will give you a series of understandings about that person. But it is based on a mental view that is being deciphered through your brain, your heart, your intuition and your knowledge. That can set up an uncomfortable set of circumstances, because you have taken the piece of paper and the numbers, and formulated your thoughts, ideas and opinions before you have looked at the person who is right in front of you. What should come first is the person, their heart, their body language and their presence, what is happening with them that day, what pain they hold, what their mood is and even what they are wearing. Everything about them is there in front of you. That is the first authentic view you are going to have of anyone.

If you are working with such systems, my recommendation is put the piece of paper to the side and communicate with the person first. Look in their eyes, really listen to them, hear their tone, hear what they have to say. Breathe them in and absorb them. Once you have done that, then you are ready to look at the piece of paper for confirmation of what your intuition has told you, rather than the other way around. So it is better not to start with the numbers, *'Oh, you're a this, you're a that. You're a Generator, you're a 2/4, you're a 1/5.'* Otherwise, you can get entrenched in a kind of numbering lingo jargon that creates a division between you and the person in front of you.

People are always surprised to hear that although I use the Gene Keys system for myself, for my own journey and contemplation, I do not use it in my personal life. Because even though I founded and teach the Gene Keys system, I find that I do not have a need to know what other people's profiles and designs are. I don't even know all the numbers of my children, and only vaguely remember what they are. I don't want the details to affect my interactions with them.

In the case of close, intimate relationships, it is useful to know some of the patterns that are coming up, that are being triggered in you. It is good to know the broad brush strokes, particularly at the higher level. If you are working with the Gene Keys, for instance, you can look at the Siddhis and the Gifts and it helps you to form a view of that person that is based on something very beneficial and beautiful, which can be helpful. But I caution looking into the Shadows of other people, the difficult patterns. The Shadows are for you, for your journey. Do not worry about anyone else's Shadows, just figure out your own. Then look at whatever someone brings to you, and what comes up in you.

These are delicate areas, but it is a golden rule in anything – the person first, the numbers second. If you are looking at your idea of a perfect relationship between two people, or two profiles or charts, or you are looking for a perfect group in a business, don't look at the numbers first. See who is in front of you. What are their skills? What are their feelings? Do they actually relate to each other? These are basic human principles, but it is easy to lose sight of them when you are involved in systems of thought and understanding. And this can be applied across many things.

Sometimes we can forget the basic, essential human components of interaction, of dialogue, and what is essentially love. How is the love flowing through this person? Where might it be blocked? Where might it need a bit more listening to?

The system should support the intuition, the intelligence and the chemistry that are alive between you and another, but it should not lead the way. The first thing to do is to listen to the person. Be with them without the profile or the chart. Bring it in for deeper insight later if you wish, but even that is not essential. What is essential is your ability to relate to another person with openness, with an open heart and an open mind.

Many of the people in my life do not know what I do. Some of my friends know that I do something a bit 'alternative', but they do not know the details or that it involves Hologenetic Profiles. I will most likely tell them if they ask, but I am not bothered if they don't. I am just there as their friend and I don't need a piece of paper, a chart, a profile or anything like that to enhance my understanding of the relationship. It is there in the air between us, and that is enough. And, sometimes, when you know the basic principles that underlie all profiles and charts, you can detect one of those patterns at work or have a hunch about it. You don't need a profile to confirm it, because you are seeing it live in person, and you know then how to respond in a compassionate and empathic way.

If you are engaged in the study of any of these systems for understanding human nature, or any psychological tool at all, it is important to remember the systems themselves, their numbers, and their language, exist to improve our skills of empathy and listening. They are for enabling us to open our hearts more, and to be more sympathetic, more resonant, and more compassionate towards others, and also towards ourselves.

PERFECTLY IMPERFECT

It is important for all seekers after the truth to know that we are all imperfectly perfect. We would all like to be perfect in some way, but we are not. So don't try to be perfect. It is a mistake that many of us make at some point, and a path that could lead us to become righteous, sanctimonious even.

It can be that our thoughts are virtuous and clear, we are doing a lot of yoga and meditation, and we don't allow any negativity into our life. We become very pure and it is all very wonderful. And then we take pride in our perfect role-model nature because we think we are really doing well. But when you are perfect, every single cell of your body will shine with truth and light. You will become an avatar. You will become like Christ. When that happens, you will know it and everyone else around you will know it! There will be no doubt or fear when it occurs, and it will occur to every single one of us at some point in our evolution. Because of that certainty we can just be where we are.

We are human and we are also divine, yet in some spiritual circles or communities that playfulness, that naughtiness, that rascal-ness can be lacking. Our sense of humour, the ability to laugh at ourselves, to see the imperfections and not take ourselves too seriously is very important. We strive for perfection, but of course we forget to be perfect or, secretly, when no one's looking, we do something that isn't perfect. So it is important to just be who we are and not pretend that we are perfect.

There are many masters that you can contemplate, but one of my great contemplations is on the Christ: What did he do to get like that? What a beautiful thing to have every single cell of your being radiant and pure, and to hold that in your inner consciousness. We are like that underneath, but we also have karma, and our work is to purify that.

So just be who you are. Be completely authentic with your shadow self as well as your crown of love. Be perfectly imperfect – there is real beauty in that.

 ZEN TEA PARTY

I am a lover of tea. Sometimes I just like to watch the steam that comes off it. For my birthday one year, I decided to hold a tea party and invited a group of friends. It was going to be a beautiful day, so I took all the sofas from the house out into the garden and onto the lawn. I set up a special area with my ceremonial tea things, and decorated the table with flowers and exquisite items that were important to me. I chose a really special tea, and everything was prepared beautifully. I had the notion of a lovely event outside in the autumn sunshine.

My son and my wife both made amazing cakes, and my friends also brought cakes and all sorts of delicious things. There were many children and nine dogs, who chased each other around the garden. I planned that we would all go for a walk and then come back and have tea together. It was wonderful. It is always wonderful to be with those you love, especially in glorious weather like that.

When the moment came, I invited everyone to sit down and have some tea, but people were drifting in and out and milling around. Some were doing things in the kitchen, preparing food and drinks and putting the final touches to the cakes, and so there wasn't really a great focus on the tea. I realised quickly that this wasn't going to go quite the way I had planned. I had imagined that we might all quietly sit down, and I would say a little prayer, and serve the tea, and there would be a kind of sanctity around it. But it didn't go that way at all.

So, I just said my little internal prayer quickly to myself, and then I allowed things to unfold as they would. People came and went. It was mostly just children in the beginning, because the adults were busy. I didn't want to over-orchestrate it, so I just started serving the tea in little cups and offering it around. Children of all ages were trying it and enjoying it, and the teenagers too.

Then the cakes came out and there was nowhere to put them except on my tea table. So I was cutting them and serving them to everyone, and pouring the tea as well. The cake got everywhere, my beautiful Zen tea table was covered in cake, and then the dogs were coming and eating it. It was a beautiful lesson in Zen, and actually the first time I had ever offered tea to a group. It was wonderful how it worked out. I felt very blessed to have all those people there. It was a very special event.

The moral of the story is not to have an expectation, or, if you do have an expectation, be willing to surrender it instantly, perhaps for something far better.

DIVINE LILA

In England, we don't have many large mountains and certainly none with consistent snow, so if you want to go skiing, you need to go further afield. One year, we headed to France for a family skiing holiday. It was hundreds of miles to drive there, about sixteen hours without stops. I set off on the journey with my three children and a friend of theirs. My wife was going to fly to Lyon, and we were going to pick her up there and then carry on to the mountains, but in the middle of France the car broke down on the motorway. Then out of that came a whole series of events, and I realised quite quickly that we were in a *lila* – a lovely Sanskrit word that the Indians have, which means a divine play.

A *lila* is like a divine envelope that the gods give you – you open the envelope and find yourself in a play. The play has a beginning, a middle and an end, and it can turn out to be large or small. You get a little rehearsal, and then a karmic play unfolds and acts itself out, and your karma unravels according to the *lila*. Life itself is a *lila*.

This particular *lila*, once we opened the envelope, was interesting. We were stuck, broken down on the motorway, so I rang the local roadside rescue service and a man came to help. He towed the car away on his trailer, and left us in the middle of nowhere. It was a Sunday, and everything was closed in France. And so we waited there. Then I called our British roadside rescue service, to discuss our plight with them. I had to negotiate my way through a whole process – navigating their rules, and trying to find a solution and a way of being rescued.

They were going to get us a hotel in the middle of nowhere, and it was a very nice area of France, but everyone just wanted to get to the mountains and start the skiing holiday, especially the children, who had been excited for weeks about it. So I told them not to worry, and I was determined to get us all there by the end of the day.

The next complication was that we still had to get to Lyon, to meet my wife. In the end, we got there by taxi. It was a long way and very expensive. The *Iila* continued and finally we got to the mountains at the end of the day, after a long drive, but everyone was delighted to get there.

Our week of skiing was wonderful, but I was trying to work out how we were going to get home. The car was 300 miles away and broken down, somewhere in the middle of France, so I spent a lot of time on the phone trying to organise everything. They always seemed to call me when I was on a ski lift or in some awkward place high up on the mountain with the wind blowing, and the person would be saying, '*I can't hear you,*' and I'd say, '*Well, I'm on the top of a mountain!*'

The car was supposed to be towed somewhere to be fixed, but the days went by and nothing happened. Until finally they got the car to a garage. We were skiing, and having a lovely time, and waiting for news. I was wondering how we were going to get home, but I wasn't worrying about it, because I knew it was a *Iila*, so I knew it would have its ups and downs, and lots of phone calls.

Then it got to Friday and the end of the week. Still the car hadn't been fixed, and we were leaving on Saturday, so I was having to think fast. I was looking into taking a hire car all the way to Calais, on the coast of France, but then we didn't want to take a French hire car into the UK.

I looked at taking a ferry, and then taxis with all our bags and ski equipment, but it wasn't going to be easy. And trying to hire two cars on a Sunday was proving impossible – on Easter Sunday of all days. There were very few car rentals open, except at the airports. The *lila* was doing its dance.

I continued trying to arrange everything, and everyone I spoke to agreed that it was something of a nightmare. Then at the very last moment on the Friday afternoon, the garage finally phoned to say that they had diagnosed the problem with the car and had fixed it. We had been thinking that even if they had diagnosed it, it would take a week at least to fix it. But suddenly it turned out that they had actually fixed it, which was great, but then it meant that I had to cancel everything that had been arranged and rebook all the original plans. So I did all that. Thank goodness for modern technology!

So our journey continued. The car was fine, but all that time the *lila* had been playing. When we finally got back to England, the moment we arrived, I had the distinct feeling that the *lila* was done with us. No more phone calls and negotiations, no more wondering how we were going to get back or what was going to happen next. The envelope was closed. The *lila* was gone. It was done.

This is such a good metaphor for all of our lives. We are all in these *lilas*, particularly when life throws us a curveball or a challenging situation. That one wasn't very challenging really, but it was the kind of thing that can make you worry. And I don't want you to have to worry. I want you, like me, to realise that you are in a *lila* when it happens. It might be in your relationships, or something that comes up that is hard for you or for others. You open this unexpected envelope and then an unravelling occurs.

Even though the *Iila* is hard and may be challenging, if you can see it as a part of a play and that there is a teaching, perhaps a forgiveness and a remembering in it for you, and an acceleration of your awareness, then it is not without purpose. That is the magic of a *Iila*. When it is done with you, it is done, and you have learned what you have learned. Sometimes you learn the hard way and sometimes you learn the easy way, because you remember that it is a *Iila*.

Life is like that in itself. Each lifetime is a *Iila*, and the whole of evolution is a *Iila*. It is God's play, God's letter to us. You open the envelope, take it out and it unravels step by step. All we have to do is surrender and allow it to unravel, keep our hearts open and try to keep smiling as much as possible. So take heart from the *Iila*, get the most out of it that you can, and enjoy it!

HOW TO WRITE KARMA-FREE EMAILS

Writing emails is not a very spiritual thing, you might think, but it is as spiritual as anything else. Email has brought wonderful improvements to our society. Being able to communicate with people instantly over long distances is an amazing thing, but only if we know how to use the tool well. Often, when you need to say something to someone as fast as you can, quickly dashing off a few words can often create more division than anything else. There are so many miscommunications that take place through emails. Especially when we are tired, we make the mistake of either writing too much or writing in the wrong way, using the wrong tone or the wrong language, which can create all kinds of problems.

I have a small formula to help in the construction and composition of karma-free emails. It is a kind of mnemonic, or aide memoire using the word 'email'. It makes writing and reading emails a magical practice in our lives, instead of something that we just have to do.

The first letter is E, for Empathy and Economy, and the process begins with the word empathy. An email is a way of connecting with someone. You have a message for them, you have something to deliver, so start with empathy, and you can apply this to all communication. Feel into the other person. Feel into what you are feeling. What is it you want to say? How might you best say it? Take a pause before you just rattle it off. Take a few breaths. There is a person at the other end who is going to receive that. What effect might that have on their life? They might be having a bad day. They might also be in a hurry. All you need to know is that they are another human being. That is how you begin.

You don't want to make things hard for them, so imagine that you are the one receiving the email and imagine how you would feel. It's nice to start with a greeting, *Dear Someone or Hi Someone.* Then I recommend beginning the main body of the message with a validation rather than just launching in with what you want to say. Spend a few seconds writing, *'It was great to see you the other day,'* or *'You've done really well on this,'* or *'Well done for...'* or some sort of comment that is not trite, or made up, or false, but something that validates them. It can be simple, a greeting in some form. Otherwise, it sometimes just seems rude and unempathetic to send something blunt, which goes straight into the reason for emailing. But, obviously, if you are in a chain of emails with the same person and they have been flying back and forth, that is a different situation. You are already communicating with them, so you can just go straight in.

The second E to consider is Economy. Is your message distilled clearly into a few points? Is it easy to digest? Try to condense your meaning into three points or fewer, and make those points clearly. Think them through, write them out, read them and then distill them. If you can learn how to edit your message into simple language and phrasing, it is a real gift, and a wonderful thing to teach yourself.

The M is for Meaning and Miscommunication. Think carefully about what it is you want to say, and how it could be interpreted and misinterpreted, and then assume it will probably be misinterpreted. So be clear and incisive with the words you choose.

The A is for Accuracy and also *Ahimsa.* Accuracy is about word choice. You have an opportunity to write something exact and precise and if you use too many words or the wrong words, you could easily create a miscommunication.

Ahimsa is a Sanskrit word, which means harmlessness, and this is essential in the process of writing a karma-free email. If you include anything that has negativity or can be misunderstood, you will actually be creating something that comes back to you negatively in some way, even though you may not have intended it, even if it was just a simple slip because you were in a hurry. *Ahimsa* means you treat everything with respect and you consider the feelings of others, and write in a way that is not harmful.

The I is for Inclusiveness, and it is very important. Depending on the content of your message, it could potentially cause the reader to feel alienated or negative, or it could make them feel included and positive. Sometimes you have to make a point very clearly, which may not be easy, but if it is really difficult you probably shouldn't be doing it in an email. You can apply this to text messaging as well, but essentially this is about emailing.

The other part of inclusiveness is who to include. The 'cc' feature is easy to use too liberally, but do we really need to cc so many people? If you cc someone, you are including them in the process and they are also likely to receive a hundred other emails. So, again, bring in empathy, and consider whether you actually need that extra person's input, because if you don't you are just adding to their inbox, and adding to the karma by bringing someone else into the situation. Think about the feelings of others and their situation, and don't include people unless it is absolutely essential that they see it. The more people who are involved, the more complex it will be, and then there will be more potential for miscommunication.

Finally the L is for Last chance. Before you hit the Send button, read your email back to yourself, preferably aloud. Does it have a kind tone? How does it make you feel when you read it?

Even if you don't remember to do anything else, give it a final read through to make sure it sits right. Writing an email can be a way in which you distill a lot of your own thoughts and feelings for yourself. So take your time when you do it. Don't just fire it off. Once it has gone, it has gone. Once you have hit 'Send', the karma is out there, along with the potential for miscommunication. Something that should have been simple can end up being a long and complex process, with more people involved than you needed, and you end up creating a whole web of difficulty and karma for yourself.

So take your time and be careful, considerate and conscientious when editing your emails. These days, people are so busy, and it can be overwhelming to have so much stuff coming at us. So keep things short, clear and kind. Then you and they will have a much better day.

Empathy and Economy – Validate the other person. Empathise with them and consider what effect your email might have on them. And edit, edit, edit, to reduce your message to its absolute essence.

Meaning and Miscommunication – Think carefully about the wording you use, to avoid misunderstanding.

Accuracy and Ahimsa – Be exact and precise in your use of words and don't use too many. Create something that doesn't cause harm, and that is based in kindness. It doesn't cost you anything to have a kind tone.

Inclusiveness – Write something that makes the reader feel included. Be careful when cc'ing – use only when essential.

Last Chance – Before you send it read it back to yourself, aloud, to see how it feels. This is the most important thing to remember.

THE CHAIN OF GIVING

There is an interesting story about Neem Karoli Baba, the Hindu guru and spiritual teacher, when he was holding a *darshan*, which is where the teacher, the master, gives out blessings in all kinds of ways. There was a noisy throng of people at this *darshan*, and more were arriving from all over to watch and listen, and maybe to place an offering on the altar of food, money or gifts for the teacher. The master was sitting there, laughing and talking, sharing out his blessings, words of advice and the traditional sweets that he was also known for giving out, when a poor and destitute-looking old woman appeared. She hobbled up, holding a crumpled one-rupee note in her small, thin hand. She placed it in the bowl on the altar and then, bowing, moved away to the back of the room. The master then asked for that one-rupee note to be brought to him.

In most countries a rupee is worth next to nothing. In India then, one rupee was possibly enough to feed you for a few days. But the master took this one-rupee note and gave it to a very wealthy Western devotee, saying, *'Take this and look after it. Keep it forever. It is precious.'* So the man took it and put in his pocket, and that is how the story ends. What became of it? We don't know. What became of that woman? We don't know. All we know is the story of the giving and the receiving.

There are many levels and layers and dimensions to the story, because when you give, and it is a sacrifice to give, then the giving is far more powerful. Because we are all interconnected, as all beings are deeply interconnected, when one gives selflessly in that way and it is a sacrifice, it forces the current of the universe to go on giving, creating a chain reaction.

It means that the next person has to give, then another person, and a further person has to give again. The chain continues because of the way we are all interconnected through fractal lines. The power of a tiny act of deep kindness is incalculable. You don't know what forces that offering truly brought into the world, into the universe, because the result of that giving is still going on, is still happening.

The ripples are still passing through the ocean of that giving, that selfless sacrifice. This is something to think about when you are giving or considering giving. For many of us, while giving a small amount of money here and there is kind and it is good, it is not a sacrifice. If, for example, a large sum of money came into your life and you made plans to spend it on renovating your house or something else that would bring pleasure into your life, that would be a wonderful way to spend it. But what if you decided to forego doing that in order to be able to give that money to somebody else, to direct it to another channel where you knew that money would be used really well? Then you would have sacrificed one of your desires for a selfless urge, a gesture of love, of kindness, to help another or others. It doesn't have to be money, as it can be many things. But money is a good example, because it symbolises our energy and our time.

The sacrifice may be small or large, and it can be made in many ways, but it is the sacrifice that carries the charge that creates the karmic chain reaction, and the ripples from it then come back to you. How could they not? They go out and they come back, and they cleanse your karma. This is why love and service, divine service, is one of the greatest spiritual paths.

One act of divine service is worth weeks, perhaps months or more of pure insight meditation. It transmutes 'the forgetting' inside us and allows us to remember more.

We feel the lift of that grace through our giving to another being, another creature or a plant. Even the smallest of acts, such as rescuing an insect or nurturing something living, however tiny, contain a power that is incalculable. You cannot compare it to anything that happens on the political stage of humanity.

The tiniest acts sometimes carry the greatest consequences far beyond our lives, far beyond our understanding. There is great beauty in the phrase *Philos Anthropos,* which is the love of humanity shown through selfless giving. It is the love that is in humanity, the loving heart of humanity allowed to express itself freely. This is something to contemplate when you see those less fortunate than you.

SURVIVAL OF THE KINDEST

It is interesting that out of the different subgroupings of early humans, only one type of hominid survived and that is us, *Homo Sapiens*, which means 'wise man'. When you look at the world, humans do not seem very wise, so why are we the ones that survived?

Everyone has heard of 'survival of the fittest', an idea attributed to Charles Darwin. However, Darwin's original insight has been much misunderstood. In truth he favoured a more altruistic hypothesis. He tied the success of human evolution to the evolution of compassion. This is the idea that we survived not because we were the most aggressive, but because we were the kindest. Of all those early ancestors, we were the most inclined to care for each other. And there is evidence for 'survival of the kindest' in skeletons from early ancestors who were disabled, injured or sick and had clearly been looked after by their tribe.

There is also evidence that our branch of the species interacted successfully with other branches. So it was through taking the risk of communicating with strangers, even with those who may have seemed very different from us, that we were able to build bridges between different racial and tribal groupings.

This view of openness, care and compassion for each other changes the view that early humans were essentially selfish. And still, now, even though we are prone to violence when we feel threatened, and some of the traits we know about ourselves can be very unpleasant, underneath it all we are kind. It is clear that this is a strength rather than a weakness because love is actually the force that ensures survival.

Kindness is an extraordinary power. You can put it into practice for yourself and see what happens. Go through your day and be extra kind and considerate. Maybe it is being open to a stranger, or reaching out to someone you have not seen in a while or to someone you know who is suffering. It could be giving something to someone, or the gift of your time by just listening to them, even caring for plants or creatures in your garden or something simple like rescuing a bee or a spider.

You could try being extra kind for a day as an experiment. Perhaps put some things off in your day to make space for it or bring kindness into your work through your attitude. Then see how the day choreographs itself and how it feels as you watch the forces of that day spinning around. Then, at the end of the day, think back on what unfolded and consider the power of kindness. You will see that you are connecting with the very roots of your humanity, of our humanity. What will ensure our survival as we move through very uncertain times is that we are open to each other, we listen to each other and we care for those in need. This is what makes us so awesome. And changing the way you look at life and the things you do, even in small ways, will mean that you can soften even more.

We can speak words of kindness, and let that kindness resonate through our voices as genuine feeling coming from inside us. Open to this possibility, and perhaps together we can tune in to the currents of what it means to truly thrive as a species, even in times of change.

Our ancestors also faced massive changes, huge climactic questions and difficulties. The ones who survived were those that were the most adaptable and the best at communicating. The best way to communicate is through kindness.

CHAPTER 7

FINDING THE RADIANCE

The gift of inner radiance comes to us through finding beauty and connection, and we can find it when we experience the peace, exquisiteness and splendour of nature. Divine and sacred beings emanate that inner light and are surrounded by it.

The poet Keats said, 'Beauty is truth, truth is beauty,' and we can say the same of radiance. There is radiance in truth, and truth in radiance, and it is there that we can find the rapture of awakening.

PURPLE DAWN

In springtime, out in the woods that surround my childhood home in England, you can see clouds of blueish purple flowers called bluebells. They are native to Western Europe, but their stronghold is in the British Isles and they are found in ancient woodland, along hedgerows and in fields. They are exquisite and radiant.

Human auras absorb energy signatures through light, and I love to immerse myself in the vibration and light of the bluebells, inhaling their purple energy into my body and absorbing it through my eyes. It fulfils some deep need of my bio-system to experience this frequency, and I know it will have a wonderful effect on the rest of my day.

So if you can, rise early, drink the nectar of the sunrise, of the landscape, of flowers, of plants, of birds, and the light through the trees. It is rapture, it is heaven.

SACRED COMPOST

People often ask if there is any particular practice that I do. Of course, contemplation is my main practice, but that is something I do all of my day – it is my whole life. The only practice that I do specifically is going outside and connecting with the sun at sunrise. I use incantations, sometimes prayers, and various mudras, and I draw the sun into different aspects of my being and my body. It is a very precious thing that I love to do, and it is extremely powerful to saturate yourself with that morning energy of the sun.

My house is set among fields in the countryside, and the sun rises on one side of the garden exactly where the compost area is. There are two big compost bins which are constantly filled with kitchen scraps, and we have chickens, which shuffle it all around and spread it everywhere, along with their droppings. So it is quite a smelly area, but also natural and rich, and it is where I go to do my morning sessions with the sun.

All around me is a rich smell of compost and rotting food. It is everywhere and I end up standing in it too. The only place where I can see the sunrise properly is next to that pile of fetid stuff. On the other side of it is an old stone wall and a field with cows in it. The cows seem to really love it when I do 'The Holy Incantation of Solace', which is a wonderful set of movements and words that invoke higher forces and bring them into your being. If you don't already know it, it is worth finding out about and trying, as it is very powerful. If you do it regularly, every morning or even every evening, it will become imprinted in your being.

The mudras imprint into you powerfully, along with the equally powerful but simple words and movements. The more you know them deep inside, the more you can drop into the Solace itself and really feel those emanations. You are also sending it out to people in the world who really need it, so it is a really lovely thing to do, and I always do it with the rising sun. The cows come and cluster up right next to where I am doing it. They love it. They seem to like the energy and I guess they like having someone there, as they want to come close and almost snuggle up to me while they are sniffing and snorting and pooing. So I will be in the middle of saying, *'May Solace abound in the world...'* and there is a defecating sound, and I think, *'Ahh, there it is!'*

So as the sun rises, I am there with the compost and the cows, and we are in a metaphorical dance of life together. And it is a great symbol, in that it really does not matter where you decide to do your sacred practice. It does not have to be in a beautiful temple with candles, incense and nice things on the wall. It can be anywhere and in any situation. You can bring the presence of this sacred practice into the most unusual, and even the most difficult of places.

BREAD OF HEAVEN

The mountains of Rila in Bulgaria are absolutely breathtaking. It is a place of many dimensions. The first time I went there it was May and I was on a pilgrimage. I was staying in a big cabin, about 6,000 feet up. On my first day there, I woke at four in the morning, and as I lay there in my bed I could hear a woman singing, which I thought was odd. But then it came to me that there were seven lakes among those mountains, and the sound of the voice was the mountains and the lakes calling me. So I decided I would go outside and follow it.

There was snow on the ground and it was very cold, so I put on warm clothes and went outside. The light from the stars hanging over the mountains made a glittering trail on the snow. I followed the sound of the voice through the dark, picking my way through the ice fields, through rocks and a bog. Finally, after about half an hour, I came to a lake sparkling in the starlight. It was beautiful.

After a while the dawn light began to appear, and all around my feet purple crocuses were glowing in the first light of the day. It was absolutely intoxicating. I sat on a rock and watched the sunrise. I started to cry with the intensity of the experience, being there in that place and seeing the light. It felt as if I had been gathering the bread of heaven all night and all through the dawn. I had an overwhelming feeling of good news, as if there were only optimism about the future and about the now. It was all good news, exceptional news of what is coming and what is certain.

We look at the planet today, and people are worrying about this and that. But I tell you, the news is good. And that was what welled up in me, the feeling of gratitude that I am a messenger who brings only good news, like the person who delivers flowers to people, only passing on good news and seeing people's faces and hearts light up. I hope that you can experience some of this feeling, and may this bread of heaven be yours, because it will be one day, and soon.

THE MYSTIC ROSE

I love roses. They are the most exquisite flowers, and they release an aroma of love. Roses grow in many countries but England is especially known for beautiful old-fashioned roses that have a most amazing fragrance. There is nothing quite like an old English Rose, the ancient type, a mystic rose.

I often go out to my garden and pause by the roses. There are some lovely red ones just near where we park the car. So whenever I come home I stop and take a moment to smell them. It is intoxicating just to be near them. They only flower for six weeks of the year, and then they are gone, which brings to mind the old saying, *'Take time to smell the roses along the way.'* It is so good to give yourself those moments, those magical pauses in the day.

The rose has a distinctly feminine quality. In England we call a fair English maiden an 'English rose'. Happily for me, I married an English rose, so I am doubly happy. My house is also named after roses. At home I am surrounded by roses and their wonderful scent. Sometimes, I drop rosebuds into hot water in the mornings to make tea, and release their lovely fragrance. The rose of course is an emblem of love. It always has been and always will be.

May the Love of the Mystic Rose be yours too.

THE PASSING OF SAINT COLUMBA

Saint Columba was an early Christian saint who, in the sixth century, sailed from the north of Ireland to the Isle of Iona, a magical island in the Western Isles of Scotland. There, he founded Iona Abbey, and the story of his life and the miracles he performed were recorded by Adomnán, who was the Abbot of Iona a hundred years later.

This tale of Saint Columba's passing is taken from that collection of stories, 'The Life of Saint Columba'. It is a wonderful book, because it contains so many stories, some describing big miracles, and some just minor events, which add authenticity to it.

Iona is a very small island and only about a hundred people live there. It is not an easy place to get to, but many pilgrims make the journey to see the abbey, and to experience the sacredness of the place. There is a distinct aura the moment you arrive on the island. It is a very special place, and Saint Columba was obviously an extraordinary man. This tale of his passing is simple and moving.

Although Saint Columba was very old, he still wanted to be involved in the working of the abbey, and to support the monastic community and the people, right up to the end of his life. On this day his closest disciple, Diarmid, pushed him to the other side of the island in a cart, which was the time when Saint Columba famously blessed the island and all the people. A stone cross was erected at the place where he made the blessing, and it still stands there today. That blessing is said to be what creates the holiness there.

As Diarmid was pushing him in the cart, Saint Columba explained to him that the Lord had given him permission to leave, and that he was ready to go. He had been intending to pass at Easter, but then he had not wanted to sully that festival with sadness, so he had waited. He then revealed that he would be leaving the next day at midnight, and that Diarmid must not tell anyone else. At this news, his disciple wept.

In the abbey that same morning, Saint Columba had been looking up at the rafters, and his face had lit up in an inexplicable way when he was praying. His monks asked him afterwards what had happened. Saint Columba said that an angel had come, filling the abbey with its presence, and had then left through the tower. It had come to reclaim a loan that had been given to humanity. But the monks did not know what he had meant until the next day, when they realised that the loan was Saint Columba's soul.

The following day, when it was approaching midnight and the bell was ringing to call the monks to prayer, Saint Columba hastened into the abbey as fast as he could. The candles had not yet been lit, so it was too dark to see properly. His closest disciple, Diarmid, who knew what was going to happen, followed him in but could not see him, so he called out for him, 'Where are art thou, my father?' He pushed his way through the abbey, feeling for the pews and made his way to the altar, where he found his master lying close to death.

Diarmid called to the monks to gather around, and they held the master as he was departing. Then Saint Columba gave his final blessing. He could not speak, so he placed his hand on the monks, and smiled. He was filled with light, and the whole place was filled with the light of his passing.

Then came a series of miracles that took place over the following three days, as they buried him and did all the rites of passing.

One of his monks had said to Saint Columba that when he died all the people from the north-west of Scotland and Ireland would come and celebrate his life and passing. But Saint Columba had replied that it would not happen. He made a prophecy that it would be only monks from Iona, just his close friends, who would be able to celebrate his life and burial. And as it happened on the night that he died, a huge thunderstorm arose, a terrible storm that cut off the island so that no one could get through. So it was only the monks of Iona who were able to perform the three days of rites with the body of the saint.

And there are other accounts of that same night. A saint on the east coast of Ireland, a well-known sage, had a vision of Saint Columba passing, and he told all his monks that he was sure that Saint Columba had departed that night. There were also many reports from fishermen and people working in the fields who saw a huge pillar of light in the sky at around midnight. They would have been out working late, because in Northern Scotland in June the light lingers long. Many different people recounted seeing this spectacle of light when the great man departed.

Saint Columba was a very humble man and this simple story of his passing shows that the great teachers know exactly when they will depart, because our lives are measured exactly to every second. And those who are truly in tune with the rhythm of the inner life can always feel the timing of the coming and the going of the life force, not just in themselves, but also in others.

A beautiful story tells of the day before his passing. After Saint Columba had blessed the island, he was resting by the cross, when a white horse came by with a cart. It was the horse that was used to move provisions across the island.

Several monks reported that the horse approached Saint Columba, rested its head in his lap, and started weeping. When the attendants tried to draw the horse away, he stopped them, telling them to let the horse grieve. He knew that the horse understood that his master would be leaving very soon, and he remarked to his closest disciple, how extraordinary it was that the Lord's creatures could know such a thing, when most humans did not. He then blessed the horse.

If you feel interested in this early Christian saint, you might like one day to visit the Isle of Iona and feel his presence. It has a very specific and pure energy, a white light. Or perhaps you could just connect with that energy and breathe it into your soul, and be lifted and inspired by someone who lived well over a thousand years ago in a remote part of north-west Scotland, but who had a vast impact, just through his simple devotion to Christ and his teachings.

The spirit of Christ and the spirit of those higher celestial energies lived inside him and inside those who surrounded him and worked with him – the raiment of the master.

These wonderful tales of his life and the miracles that happened around him remind us of another reality, another time. But it is our reality and our time as well. These things are alive and possible, particularly in the world that we see today, where we worry so much about the future of our species and the planet. And yet, underneath everything are a mission, a pattern and a reason, and if we can stay connected to that, we stay connected to the source of all being. That is the beauty of these simple, inspirational and uplifting stories. The blessing of Saint Columba be upon us all.

THE SACRED TOUCH

There are so many opinions and so much charge around Christ, about that one man. For me, Christ's inner spirit and the many layers, tapestries and stories that surround him are here for our contemplation, for us to harvest the fruits of those stories and understand what they mean for us.

One story that I have contemplated is the story of Christ moving through the marketplace, which is in itself a wonderful metaphor. That being of light was moving through the bustling marketplace full of people buying and selling, busy in their lives, and that one light moved slowly through it all, touching people, connecting and seeing them awakening. One woman came up behind him in the crowd, wanting to be close to him. She was in great need of healing, so she lightly touched his cloak, hoping to be relieved of her suffering. In awe of him, she wanted to touch that purity for herself, and in doing so she was healed. Christ felt the healing power move through him. He stopped immediately and called out, *'Who touched me?'* The crowd fell silent. Again he asked, *'Who touched me?'* And one of his disciples said, *'Lord, we are crammed in here in the marketplace, and many of us are touching you.'* But Christ said, *'No. Somebody touched me.'*

The woman came forward and said, *'I did, and I have been healed.'* And Christ saw her, saw right into her, and he blessed her. He blessed her for her huge faith. She was waiting for that moment of awakening by the master. One can imagine this being a turning point, after which her entire life changed, and she became a great, awakened soul. The master comes, and sometimes we have to reach out with faith. It is a beautiful story.

I often think about a being like Christ or Buddha, or one of the great avatars, as not being a single being, but a collective soul, an oversoul. When they come, they are clothed in their raiment of light, and that woman became a part of the light of his raiment, part of Christ. I feel that they were destined to come together, for her to touch him, and for him to heal and awaken her. But it was not really 'he' who awakened her, it was the transmission of the light moving through the drama of human life. In that moment they became one being extending itself through time and space. Even after Jesus died, that being continued through its incarnation cycles. The central part incarnated perhaps just that one time, or perhaps it has come again in another form in some other *yuga*, some other great earth cycle. But the cycles continue for the Apostles and for those people to whom miracles occurred, like the woman in the marketplace.

I found myself travelling along that woman's emanation, her incarnational thread, and it came out in Mother Julian, the great medieval mystic. She is also one of the great ecstatics that I discuss in the Ecstatics series – talks that I gave about those who have awakened the higher consciousness of the heart. I like to think that Mother Julian was that woman in the marketplace who touched Christ's raiment, that soul who had the huge experience of Christ, which led to the arrival of her great, higher soul. She then continued with that Christ-light pouring through her, and through her cycles of incarnation, until her journey came to a glorious crescendo in itself.

Sometimes when we contemplate these mysteries, they continue to open and reveal themselves. Consider the import of this simple story and imagine it was you. Imagine you were there. Imagine you were Christ. Imagine you were that woman. And if you look up Mother Julian in the Ecstatics series, you will hear where and how the story continues.

I AM ETERNAL

At the end of the year in the Northern Hemisphere, when we in the West celebrate Christmas and the winter solstice, there is a paradox that many of us struggle with. It is the manic, materialistic rush that has become Christmas, and it happens just when our bio-rhythm is ready to slow down and we want to go within and, perhaps, celebrate the sacred and the holy in a more contemplative way. The paradox is that our society has created an opposing situation that makes many of us feel exhausted and stressed.

It is important to remember what Christmas is really about, of course, and many of us do when we finally get to Christmas Eve, and we suddenly sigh, when the presents have been bought, the tree is up, and all the festivities have been arranged. There is great magic in that all coming together. We have collected all the trappings of our culture and brought them to the Christmas festival. But we also bring great focus on all that is best in us, and that is what Christmas is about. For me, Christmas time is always a reminder of the inner light, because we gather together to remember the life of one man, Jesus. Whether you are a Christian or not, this man was an extraordinary person. He never for a moment lost touch with the purity of his heart. He has become an emblem, an icon, a symbol, for so many, of all that is best in us.

When I go within, I am reminded that each one of us is eternal. We are eternal beings. When we look at what is happening in the world outside, we worry about it all and take it so seriously, whether it is the political stage, war, poverty, homelessness, global warming or any number of catastrophes around the world. Countless communities and individuals are suffering.

Even people with everything they need are in deep pain and mental anguish. Everywhere, people are suffering. Yet behind it all we are eternal. Not we, humanity, but the spirit that lives in each of us, the light that shines in our eyes, is eternal.

The message is simple: we are eternal. Quietly say to yourself, *'I am eternal. I am eternal. I am eternal. I can never die.'* Time marches on, but it does not touch that eternity. Nothing that happens here touches that eternity, that pure Christ state. Nothing can touch it. It remains unsullied and pure and it remains within us, within each of us and all things. And that is the most important thing to remember at Christmas, or at any time of year – that we are eternal.

SAINT BRIGID

Ancient sacred sites, of which Cornwall in England has many, are beautiful places to visit and are mostly undisturbed. They are places to go and commune with the wild spirits that live there. Places of purity and purification. Contemplative places.

Several sacred springs and holy wells around the British Isles bear the name of Saint Brigid, a fifth-century Celtic saint, and Ireland's most well-known female saint. Some of these ancient sites were also traditionally sacred to Brigid or Bride, the pagan goddess of fertility and nature, and Saint Brigid was also known for her love of poetry, healing and a deep respect for nature.

I visited one of Saint Brigid's wells when I was in Cornwall. The sacred spring had a little stone house built over the top of it, with beautiful mosses growing in the stone, and the trees nearby were adorned with brightly-coloured strips of fabric and ribbons that people had tied on. Traditionally Celtic areas like Ireland and Cornwall are often home to holy wells and sacred springs, and you will likely find a tree nearby with rags and ribbons tied on the branches. Known as clootie trees, clootie wells or rag wells, these are Celtic wishing trees.

The tradition is to dip the strip of fabric into the sacred water and then tie it onto a branch while making a healing wish, and perhaps making a pledge in return. Often, there are crystals and other offerings too. They are special and beautiful places, magical places that people care for, and use to connect with the ancient spirit of the land and the healing powers of the water.

Just as people tie ribbons, cords and wool on those trees to represent their wishes across the invisible divide, the Gene Keys community creates cords and connections with each other across the world in their shared journey of awakening, moving through the teachings of the Gene Keys. It is beautiful.

FRAGMENTS OF LIGHT
CHAPTER 8

THE GOOD PRAYER

*'The Good Prayer' was written in 1900
by a Bulgarian spiritual teacher called
Peter Deunov, who was also known to his
followers as Master Beinsa Douno.*

*There are many translations of 'The Good Prayer'.
This one is by Ernestina Staleva and
Antoaneta Krushevska, from their book
'Prayers, Formulas, Devotional Songs'.*

THE GOOD PRAYER

Merciful Heavenly Father,
Who has bestowed upon us life and health
That we may rejoice in you.
We pray to you to send us your spirit,
To guard and protect us in every evil and deceptive thought.

Teach us to do your will,
To sanctify your name and to glorify you always.
Enlighten our spirits and guide our hearts and minds,
That we may keep your commandments and precepts.

With your presence, inspire your pure thoughts within us,
That they may guide us to serve you with joy.

Our lives, which we dedicate to you
for the good of our Brethren and neighbours,
Bless you, O Lord.
Help us and sustain us,
That we may grow in your knowledge and wisdom,
Learn from your words and abide in your truth.

Guide us in everything
Which we think and do in your name,
That it may be for the manifestation
Of your kingdom on earth.

Nourish our souls with your heavenly bread,
And fortify us with your power,
That we may be ever advancing in your eyes.

And, as you bestow upon us all your blessings,
So grant us your love as well, to become our eternal Lord.
For yours is the kingdom, the power and the glory,
Forever and ever.

Amen

ALL FRAGMENTS IN ALPHABETICAL ORDER

OTHER BOOKS BY RICHARD RUDD

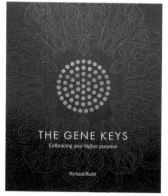

THE GENE KEYS
Embracing your higher purpose

Richard Rudd

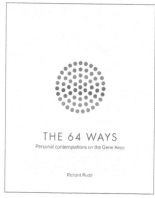

THE 64 WAYS
Personal contemplations on the Gene Keys

Richard Rudd

THE GENE KEYS
GOLDEN PATH

GENIUS
A Guide to your Activation Sequence

Richard Rudd

THE GENE KEYS
GOLDEN PATH

LOVE
A Guide to your Venus Sequence

Richard Rudd

THE GENE KEYS
GOLDEN PATH

PROSPERITY
A Guide to your Pearl Sequence

Richard Rudd

THE GENE KEYS
GOLDEN PATH

HARMONY
A Guide to your Star Pearl

Richard Rudd

DARE TO BE DIVINE
A journey into the miraculous

Richard Rudd

THE SEVEN SACRED SEALS
Portals to Grace

Richard Rudd

genekeys.com/books

OTHER BOOKS BY RICHARD RUDD

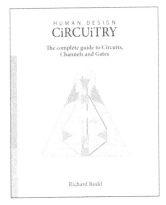

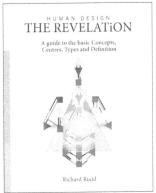

genekeys.com/books

Printed in the USA
CPSIA information can be obtained
at www.ICGtesting.com
LVHW071927131023
761059LV00006B/12